# The *Bible* Teaches

# ACTING IN LEADERSHIP

I0560458

## Scott M. Carter

Scott M. Carter Publishing

Forest Lake, Minnesota

Scott M. Carter/Scott M. Carter Publishing

Forest Lake, MN 55025

www.scottmcarter.com  (publishing permissions)

Book Layout ©2017 BookDesignTemplates.com

Cover Design: selfpubbookcovers.com/JohnBellArt

The *Bible* Teaches Acting In Leadership/ Scott M. Carter. —1st ed.

ISBN 979-8-9879170-4-6

Thank you to my incredible wife Lisa, my family, and my friends who support my efforts to continue writing with a focus on serving others. Thank you to everyone who inspires me to act in leadership, and thank you to my readers who support my works.

*Acting in leadership is what makes a person a leader.*
~Scott M. Carter.

# Contents

# Introduction

## *A Bible-based book by me?*

How did someone like me end up writing a book about the *Bible*?

I grew up in Forest Lake, Minnesota, a small town 27 miles north of our state capital, Saint Paul. My parents moved there in the 1950s. At that time, our quaint little town was a mix of homes with full-time occupants and small cabins around the lake that were only occupied in the summer months. In the 1960s and 1970s, living there was considered "up north." People said you were insane if you wanted to live there and drive 27 miles into the city to work. One would have thought people were still traveling by horse and buggy.

Our home had a lake directly out the back door, a thing of magic and beauty with sandy beaches and wildlife everywhere. Just a few minutes' walk would bring us to the city park, which had a bait shop and candy store combined.

In contrast, Highway 61 was directly out our front door. When I say, "Highway 61 was just out our front door," I mean literally. It was twenty-five feet from our front steps to the curb. Highway 61 was one of the leading commerce routes from Duluth, Minnesota, to pretty much anywhere south of Duluth.

Duluth was, and still is, a major shipping port for commerce. Semi-trucks went south and north past our front door all day and night. The train tracks that ran the same route to Duluth were not more than a few hundred feet west of this heavily traveled highway.

Locomotives dragging hundreds of cars filled with iron ore, known as taconite, and other cars filled with dangerous liquids roared through our little town. These trains did not putt along; they flew by at high speeds. Just one of the hundreds of cars filled with taconite can weigh as much as 140,000 tons. Yes, you read that right.

During the day, we would put pennies on the train tracks so they would get flattened. We would stand not more than ten or fifteen feet away and count the number of cars as they raced by. The noise was deafening, but those things don't bother you when you are a kid. We would lose interest in counting the cars after the number exceeded 100; the string of roaring wheels seemed to go on forever; countless 140,000-ton cars filled with little metal balls of iron ore. We'd collect the little metal pellets that spilled out of the cars and use them in our slingshots.

Our home was built in 1915. In the 1960s, air conditioning was not common. There were a few window units here and there, but certainly not the central air that is so common today. Only one home in our neighborhood had a window air conditioner: the Barnier family.

During the summer, all the windows in our house were wide open. Semi-trucks roared by all night, and at least one large, never-ending train would pass through. Our entire house would shake. If you were awake when one of these trains rumbled through town, you could feel your bed shake and hear the loud clickety-clack of hundreds of metal wheels resonating through the house.

When my parents bought that home in 1964, I was three years old. Our dad worked two jobs. By day, he was a laborer working on the printing presses at the Pioneer Press Dispatch. By night, he would tend the bar at the local bowling alley. When he wasn't doing either of those things, he spent a great deal of his time socializing at the American Legion just a few blocks away. He served in the Korean War.

To me, our childhood seemed normal. It contains some of the best memories of my life. By the time my siblings and I reached our late teens and early twenties, those experiences had changed dramatically. Our parents struggled with alcohol and other challenges that many people face. Divorce was the result. At one point, our dad disappeared for three years. We had no idea where he went. When we became old enough to do so, three of us kids scattered to the wind, distancing ourselves from this toxic environment as quickly as possible, leaving our youngest brother alone with our mom to fend for themselves.

Decades later, he would share stories of their struggles and what they did to survive after everyone abandoned them during that tumultuous time. Looking back now, I see how self-absorbed I was. This selfishness and self-indulgent period of my life still haunts me from time to time. I realize now that I should have been there for them, but I was not. Guilt is a powerful thing and will consume you if you let it. I wonder how different our lives might have been if we had understood the life lessons presented in the *Bible* and practiced those lessons in our lives.

The best memories of my early life did not include anything related to religion. Our dad was raised catholic. When I was young, I didn't know what that meant or what it involved; it's just what I was told. For our family, it meant going to church on Sunday and sitting in the front row. I counted the minutes until we could get the heck out of there. The only thing that separated that hour into chunks of palatable time were the sit, kneel, and stand rituals. I knew the service was getting closer to the end when people got in line to eat a little white wafer, as if they were patiently waiting for their turn to sample something at Costco.

After church, we'd promptly return home and then go on about our lives, playing outside, doing whatever. By the 1970s, that transitioned into returning home to watch All-Star Wrestling on TV. We would praise the lord, then watch grown men talk smack about their opponent and beat the crap out of each other for an hour. We experienced nothing about or related to church, faith, the *Bible*, or religion until next Sunday at 11:00 am. Like the sit, kneel, and stand ritual inside the church, the church was a routine without substance.

I had never witnessed anyone in our family read the *Bible*, nor was any understanding of the *Bible* or Christianity taught to us by our parents. Our parents did not associate with others from the church. They were barflies. Let me be very clear. I never saw a *Bible* in our house. "Good Catholics do this. Shut up and get in the car," was all I ever heard. Other than that, I never knew why we went.

The strangest component of these weekly visits to the steeple-topped building is that our mom did not attend church with us because she was raised Lutheran. Even as children, we just felt this behavior to be at odds with what common sense might tell us. If church is good for us, why isn't it good for Mom? We were not allowed to question it, so those words questioning why she didn't have to go were never uttered by any of us.

I went through all the Catholic practices, such as confirmation, first communion, and baptism. Much of it is a blur, but for the events surrounding my first communion at the age of eight, there is one memory I shall never forget.

I had to read materials, answer questions, and draw pictures. I understood none of it. As I struggled with the lessons I was supposed to be learning, I walked into the living room where my parents were sitting and asked for help. My dad yelled at me and told me to get back in the other room and stay there until I figured it out. He was angry that I asked, and I'm fairly sure some curse words were used.

Looking back, I thought it was because I had interrupted their TV show. But the reality is that neither of them could help me because they did not know or understand it themselves - a guess on my part, but a very high probability of that being the case since I'd bet my life on the fact that neither had ever read the *Bible.*

I share this with you, the reader, so you understand what part religion and the *Bible* played in my life. None of it had any meaning. That's what I meant by "someone like me" in the opening statement of this chapter. When anyone I know from the early years of my life hears I'm writing this, the reactions are fun to watch. "You? Bwaaahaaaaahaaaa!" A grin and silence from me. Then they add, "Oh wait. You're not joking, are you?" Another grin and silence from me. Then I hear, "Can I get a copy?"

Trust me, anyone who knew me in my 20s and 30s would not use the word "saint" in the same sentence with my name. They'd fear bursting into flames. Like many people, I am not proud of some of the things I did back then.

This book did not spring from a lifelong faith in anything unless making fun of people we referred to as *Bible* Thumpers is a type of faith. The only time I ever went to church as a young adult was to see a friend or family member get married. That was only a ritual precursor to attending the reception to party with friends. We thought it was awesome when we had a friend who got married in a Lutheran church. Those services only last about 30 minutes versus a Catholic wedding ceremony that can take over an hour. We called it Catholic aerobics, sit, kneel, stand, sit, kneel, stand. I've made that joke so many times, I think those words just appeared on the page without me even typing.

Perhaps you have no religious affiliation. Maybe you are a devout Christian. Perhaps you have never read the *Bible*. Maybe you have begun to read it or read most or all of it. It doesn't matter which category you fall into; you're about to learn that the *Bible* teaches acting in leadership.

I guarantee you have not seen anything like what I present in this book. How can I make that claim? In my previous two books, *There's No Such Thing As Business Leadership* and *Back To BASIC™: Acting In Leadership*, I dismantle most of the over 1,000 labels and definitions of leadership that exist today. After three years of deep research on the concept of leadership, I was able to define "what leadership means in its true essence." All of the currently existing books that talk about the *Bible* in terms of leadership use the misguided leadership labels and definitions that accumulated over the last 80 years. I will not be using any of those misplaced definitions in this book.

Here is the journey we will take together in this book.

- We will define "acting in leadership," which is significantly different than simply defining "leadership."
- We will see how leadership is fundamentally about how we behave, act, and conduct ourselves.
- We will learn that the *Bible* is something entirely different than how most people view it.
- We will learn that scientific foundational principles and universal laws of behavior exist and apply to everyone. These principles and laws tell us when we are acting in leadership.
- We will learn that all of these foundational principles and universal laws exist in the *Bible*, and they define leadership in its true essence.

I want to convey two things through this book.

1) A blueprint for acting in leadership exists. This blueprint defines leadership in its true essence. Only when a person acts in leadership are they a leader.
2) The *Bible* teaches acting in leadership. Leadership is fundamentally about how we behave and how we conduct ourselves. The *Bible* illustrates the foundational principles, universal laws, and the attributes of acting in leadership.

Second, I wanted to provide an easy and effective way for anyone to introduce the *Bible* to others by illustrating how the *Bible* teaches acting in leadership.

I am a researcher and skeptic by nature, not someone who was raised in a faith-based atmosphere. This is a good thing because it allowed me to look at the *Bible* through an objective lens. The *Bible* is one of the primary sources that helps us determine what it means to act in leadership.

This book is unlike any other *Bible*-based book you've read. Hold onto your seats, folks! Here we go.

# CHAPTER ONE

# BASIC™ Leadership Blueprint

The acronym BASIC stands for Belief, Action, Success, Insight, and Collaboration.

> ➤ Belief—Trust, Faith, or Confidence in Someone or Something.
> ➤ Action—To Take Action; Do Something
> ➤ Success—The Result from Taking Action Toward a Worthy Ideal
> ➤ Insight—The Capacity to Gain an Accurate and Intuitive Understanding
> ➤ Collaboration—Joining with Someone or Something to Produce or Create

On the following page, you'll see an image containing these five elements and an image of the Leadership Lifeline.

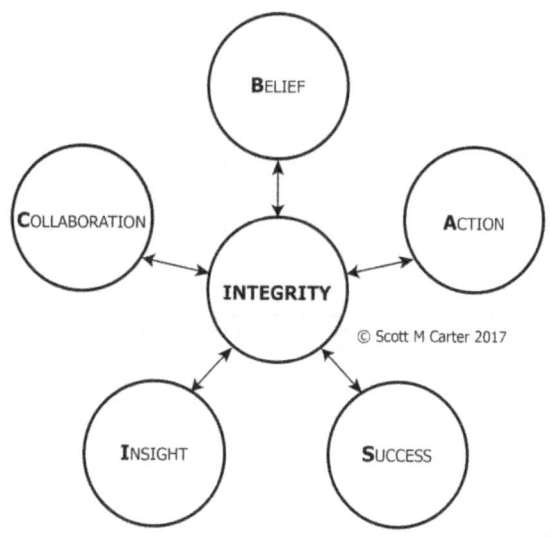

**Back to BASIC**™
**Leadership Platform**

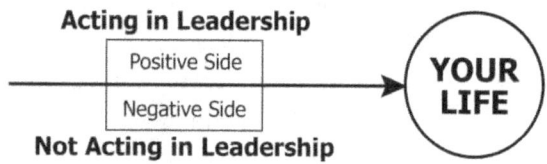

**Back to BASIC**™
**Leadership Life Line**

© Scott M Carter 2017

Success is the only component that needs a bit more clarification. Our definition of success comes from Earl Nightingale's 1957 radio broadcast: "the progressive realization of a worthy ideal."

Success is not about some end goal. It comes from taking action or not taking action, and through a combination of unsuccessful and successful attempts, we continue to progress toward something. Success is an infinite journey toward whatever you decide is your worthy ideal.

This definition is the most effective way to describe how our lives constantly progress in a forward direction and how that progression can lead to a positive outcome or a negative outcome.

These five components illustrate what happens organically in life. We constantly move around between these five components. This movement from one component to another never stops.

For instance, we act on our beliefs. Those actions create new insight, impact our beliefs, and then we take a new or different action. During that entire process, we progress into our future life.

Thoughts and beliefs are useless without action. Those actions create a progression. During that progression, sometimes we will have positive outcomes (successes) and sometimes we will have negative outcomes (non-successes). From those successes and non-successes, we gain insight. We will always be collaborating with someone or something during that progression. That's how life in general operates.

You'll notice that there is no direct path from one component to another. You cannot go directly from action to insight. In order to move from one component to another, a person must pass through the integrity hub. When a person moves from one component to another component, their belief, action, insight, progression, and collaboration must be of integrity. When the conditions of integrity have been met, then, and only then, can they move from one component to another.

Integrity: The quality of being honest and having strong moral principles; moral uprightness. The state of being whole and undivided.

Next, a person's beliefs, actions, progression, insight, and collaboration must also land (exist) on the positive side of the leadership lifeline, shown in the second image.

We can state it this way. Acting in leadership is fluid, moving from one component to another, done with integrity and existing on the positive side of the leadership lifeline. We act in leadership only when we act with integrity, and our actions land on the positive side of the leadership lifeline. Then, and only then, are we a leader in that moment.

When we look at any of the five components of the outer ring—belief, action, success, insight, and collaboration—they are the primary components of how life happens—the fundamentals of life. All five contain attributes that are both good and bad, positive and negative. Here are some examples.

## Beliefs:

People can have positive and negative beliefs. One person may believe it's okay to steal their neighbor's things (bad, negative, lacking integrity), while another may believe it is not okay to steal (good, positive, living with integrity).

## Action:

Taking the action to steal their things (bad, negative, lacking integrity). Taking the action to not steal others' things (good, positive, living with integrity).

## Success (Worthy Ideal):

For some people, a worthy ideal is to become wealthy by stealing (bad, negative, lacking integrity). For most people, a worthy ideal is to never steal (good, positive, living with integrity).

## Success (Progression):

The progression of stealing over and over again, becoming better at living that way (bad, negative, lacking integrity). The progression of continuing not to steal. Becoming better at living that way (good, positive, living with integrity).

## Insight:

Gaining insight on how to become good at stealing (bad, negative, lacking integrity). Gaining insight that stealing is bad and has consequences (good, positive, living with integrity).

*Collaborate:*

Collaborating with others to steal and gain more insight on stealing (bad, negative, lacking integrity). Collaborating with others about the consequences and effects of stealing (good, positive, living with integrity).

I could easily give you a hundred examples of both the positive and negative sides of all five components. These five components alone do not define the actions of a leader or establish anyone as a leader; they are what we all do in life. We all believe things, we all take action, we all progress forward in life, we all gain insight, and we all collaborate in one form or another.

The purpose of the integrity hub and the leadership lifeline is to filter out the bad, negative, and anything lacking the qualities of integrity. That's how easy it is to understand how the BASIC Leadership blueprint determines when a person is acting in leadership, and thereby a leader at any given time. I can sum it up with the following two statements.

> *We do not act rightly because we have virtue or excellence, but we rather have those because we have acted rightly.* ~Aristotle

Because of the philosophy of Aristotle, we can say it this way.

> *You are not a leader first, then attempt to act rightly. You act rightly; that is what makes you a leader.*
> ~Scott M. Carter

I will provide plenty of examples in upcoming chapters to illustrate exactly how the BASIC Leadership blueprint works. You will get to see it in action. It's an amazingly effective way to determine when a person acts in leadership and thereby a leader. Like I said in the introduction, you haven't seen anything like this before.

Let's gain insight into why the BASIC Leadership blueprint is significantly more effective in defining leadership than any of the over 1,000 current definitions.

# CHAPTER TWO

# Leadership Myths
# and The Loop

## *Leadership Myths*

Now that we have defined what it means to act in leadership, we can put the 1,000-plus modern-day leadership labels to the test.

Go online and complete a search on the concept of leadership. Use any language you like. Some common searches include "leadership traits and actions," "what makes a good leader?" and "what do leaders do?"

What did you find? The lists are all over the place. First, you'll notice that the traits and actions begin to repeat in different variations and as contrasting opposites. For instance, a repeating concept presented differently is "Leaders have gratitude" and "Leaders are grateful." A contrasting opposite would be "Leaders remain calm" and "Leaders don't get angry." In both instances, I've said the same thing in two different ways, creating a rise in complexity. We'll address complexity in detail in this chapter.

Second, ask yourself this question. Is anyone teaching or coaching negatively based leadership traits and attributes? For instance, is anyone telling us that leaders should not act with integrity? The answer is "no." Then why do we have the label of "unethical leadership?"

The answer is simple. The concept of leadership became associated with a position in a hierarchy and doing business, neither of which has anything to do with acting in leadership.

When we ask the question, "What does it mean to act in leadership?" the answer is significantly different from the answers derived from asking the question, "What is leadership?"

How would you answer the following questions?

➢ Can anyone act in leadership regardless of their ethnicity, race, gender, or any other categorically identifying traits or the position they hold in any hierarchy?

➢ Would acting in leadership be different for any person based on ethnicity, race, gender, other categorically identifying traits, or the position they hold in any hierarchy?

If the following holds true;

> ➢ Anyone can act in leadership regardless of their ethnicity, race, gender, any other categorically identifying traits, or the position they hold in any hierarchy, and
> ➢ Acting in leadership is not different for any person based on their ethnicity, race, gender, any other categorically identifying traits, or the position they hold in any hierarchy...

...then, why do we have all the different leadership labels associated with Black, Asian, White, Brown, Hispanic, Male, Female, and on and on?

Would acting in leadership be different for someone of Asian descent and someone of Hispanic descent?

When we say that acting in leadership is different for people based on any identity characteristic, such as ethnicity, race, gender, age, or position in a hierarchy, we end up with an unlimited number of different labels and definitions.

Where did all these labels come from? Why do they exist?

> 1. One dictionary definition of leadership ties leadership to a position in hierarchies; therefore, we associate leadership with the top level or levels of hierarchies.
> 2. Those who were studying leadership studied it in relation to the activities associated with

      operating businesses, government entities, and other hierarchical structures.

3. Because of how we viewed leadership and we studied it under the guise of how businesses, government entities, and other hierarchical structures operated, we created a boatload of leadership labels associated with positions that already had titles.

Guise means an external form, appearance, or manner of presentation, typically concealing the true nature of something. We unknowingly concealed the true nature of acting in leadership by associating it with how businesses, government entities, and other hierarchical structures operated. Here's an example of how things went awry.

We already had titles for all positions in all hierarchies. In business, the titles of CEO, Executive, and Director were already in place. Then, along came the term Leadership. We attached the label of leader and leadership to the top level of hierarchies, creating a new positional name. Instead of CEO, that person is now called a leader, based solely on that person holding a top position in the hierarchy.

Ethnicity-based labels such as Black Leadership, White Leadership, and Asian Leadership appeared because the concept of leadership became attached to a position in a hierarchy and associated with doing business. Now, instead of a Hispanic CEO, Black CEO, or

White CEO, we have a Hispanic leader, Black leader, and White leader.

We began to separate people by race, ethnicity, age, and gender. Isn't our goal to not associate people with their ethnicity, race, age, or gender and look at everyone through the lens of their actions and character?

I wasn't the first person to point this out. Experts who studied businesses for decades began to bring this to light as early as the 1960s.

If what I'm presenting is common sense, and business experts pointed this out sixty years ago, why did this attachment of leadership to positional hierarchies continue? Because no one came up with an alternative. When there is no alternative, there is no new path to take.

Without an alternative, people continued to try to define leadership. I tried and failed. Trying to define leadership is what caused over 800 different leadership labels to be created by 1989. The number of labels has now exceeded 1,000.

I changed the question. Instead of asking, "What is leadership?" I asked, "What does it mean to act in leadership?" When I did that, after three years of research, the BASIC Leadership blueprint took shape. I did not start with the acronym BASIC and then fill in the blanks. These seven components were the primary common threads across multiple cultures, thousands of miles apart, and those components have existed for thousands of years.

My book, *There Is No Such Thing As Business Leadership*, illustrates, in detail, how all of these leadership labels appeared and why. The overall premise that these over 1,000 labels and definitions are misguided is simple. Look at it this way: If I asked you, "Are ethics in life different from ethics in business?" The answer would be "no." Therefore, there is no such thing as business ethics; there are only ethics.

We can ask similar questions about ethics. And answer them quickly and confidently.

> ➢ Can anyone act ethically regardless of their ethnicity, race, gender, or any other categorically identifying traits or the position they hold in any hierarchy? The answer is "yes."
> ➢ Would acting ethically be different for any person based on their ethnicity, race, gender, other categorically identifying traits, or the position they hold in any hierarchy? The answer is "no."

Leadership cannot be different for an Asian person and a Hispanic person any more than ethics can be different for an Asian person and a Hispanic person. Do you think there is a different set of ethics for how a person should act if a person is of Asian descent versus Hispanic descent? The answer is "no." Therefore, there is no such thing as Asian ethics or Hispanic ethics. Ethics should be identical for everyone. There is no such thing as business ethics. Following this logical reasoning, acting in leadership is also the same for everyone.

In that book, I illustrated how these hundreds of labels are myths and fads. Then, I wrote the book, *Back To BASIC: Acting In Leadership*, presenting how the BASIC Leadership blueprint defines when a person is acting in leadership and, thereby, a leader.

I created an alternate path. If I had only argued against the thousands of leadership definitions and not created an alternate path, then we'd still be in the same boat. I would not have written my second, third, and fourth books if the BASIC Leadership blueprint hadn't surfaced during my research.

Now, let's ask ourselves the same questions we asked earlier. We can also answer these quickly and confidently.

> ➤ Can anyone act in leadership regardless of their ethnicity, race, gender, or any other categorically identifying traits or the position they hold in any hierarchy? Yes!
> ➤ Would acting in leadership be different for any person based on their ethnicity, race, gender, other categorically identifying traits, or the position they hold in any hierarchy? No!

If this is the case, then why do we have all the different leadership labels associated with ethnicity, race, gender, other categorically identifying traits, or the position they hold in any hierarchy? Why do we have

Black Leadership, White Leadership, Asian Leadership, Female Leadership, or Male Leadership?

Please argue your premise if you answered either of those questions differently. Start by arguing why Black Leadership is different than Hispanic Leadership. Be careful that you are not simply arguing about the number of specific ethnicities, races, or genders that hold a top-level position in any hierarchy. That's an entirely different argument.

How about "unethical leadership? "Do you think that should be a type of leadership? When someone acts unethically, can they pass through the integrity hub and land on the positive side of the leadership lifeline? The answer is "no."

No one teaches people how to act unethically and then says, "This is what leaders do." They say, "This is something leaders do not do. They do not act unethically." Acting unethically is not a leadership trait. It is a non-leadership trait. There is no such thing as unethical leadership.

By understanding how all of the over 1,000 definitions of leadership came to be and then providing an alternate, more effective way to define when a person is a leader, we can also test statements such as "leadership is influence."

Influence can be both negative and positive. A person can be influenced to do something bad or something good. The simplistic idea that "leadership is influence" falls apart. Instead, we test the person's actions against the integrity hub and the leadership lifeline. Influencing someone is an action a person takes. Influencing someone to steal fails the test for acting in leadership.

We can also rule out conditional definitions or statements such as "in order to be a leader, a person needs followers." This statement attaches a condition that can easily be debunked. The condition is "leadership requires followers." No one needs followers to act in leadership.

When we follow logical deductive reasoning, using the BASIC Leadership blueprint as our guide, the most popular labels, such as transactional leadership, transformational leadership, participative leadership, and authoritative leadership, become significantly less effective in defining what it means to be a leader. That does not mean that we cannot learn from what has been written about those labels. It means that none of them should be a type of leadership.

I know what you are feeling right now. That happened to me when I discovered how all of these misguided labels and types of leadership came to be. I felt like I had been duped and lied to for the last two or three decades. But that's not the case. It's because there was no alternative, and no one knew better.

Next, we will see how this misguided approach to defining leadership has created a level of confusion and complexity never before seen.

## The Loop of Optimal Effectiveness

Would you agree that we all want to be more effective, whether in business or life? Effective is different than efficient. I can be really efficient at some task or process without being highly effective in reaching my objective. We have been really efficient at creating leadership labels and definitions without being effective in defining leadership.

My goal is to effectively define when a person is acting in leadership. The greatest benefit I discovered is that focusing on effectiveness has led to being efficient at the same time.

After noticing this correlation, I researched the connection between effectiveness and efficiency. Sure enough, studies have been done, and there is a scientifically proven correlation. Focusing on effectiveness automatically leads to higher levels of efficiency.

Looking at effectiveness will help us understand the significance of the old approach to defining leadership and the new approach to defining when a person is acting in leadership.

We will use the Loop of Optimal Effectiveness to make our comparison. If you haven't heard of the Loop of Optimal Effectiveness before, it is because I also created this concept. It illustrates the impact that complexity has on effectiveness. An image illustrating the loop and the explanation of how the loop works are on the next page.

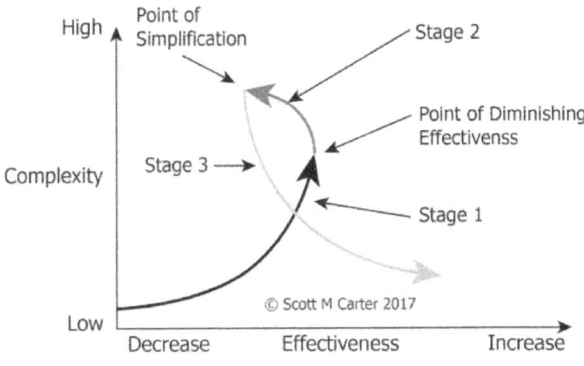

**Loop of Optimal Effectiveness**

## The three stages of complexity and effectiveness

1. Stage One: As the level of complexity rises, the level of effectiveness begins to taper off, and at some point, it has peaked and is no longer increasing.

2. Stage Two: From that point, when the level of complexity continues to rise, our ability to be effective can decrease. We go backwards.

3. Stage Three: The only way to begin moving toward increasing effectiveness is to decrease complexity, to simplify.

## Galls' Law

John Gall was an author and pediatrician who wrote about systems theory. He is best known for *Gall's Law*. From his work, we know two things with a high level of certainty.

I. A complex system that works is invariably found to have evolved from a simple system that works, and

II. A complex system that works poorly is invariably found to have evolved from a simple system that worked well.

Galls' Law helps to confirm the premise of the Loop of Optimal Effectiveness and the fact that everything in life follows the loop.

Example: We had a system for labeling all the positions in all hierarchies. It was a simple system that worked well: CEO, Executive, Manager, Laborer, etc. Then, we added the label of leader to the top positions of all hierarchies. Adding the label of leader to hierarchies created an astounding number of new hierarchical labels. We now have a more complex system for labeling positions, which works poorly, evolving from a simple system that worked well.

Something tells me that the little light bulb of logical reasoning just lit up over your head. The Bible already had titles too: Elders, Rulers, Chiefs, Guides, Kings, and Shepherds. Context changes by saying "leader."

Let's look at what happened when we attempted to define leadership. We ended up with over 1,000 different labels, including negatively based types of leadership.

Has the current approach to "defining leadership" increased or decreased in complexity? Is it high in complexity and low in effectiveness? Low in complexity and high in effectiveness? Or somewhere in between?

Has the current approach to "defining leadership" brought us closer to agreeing on what being a leader means? Is there a high level of agreement, or is there a low level of agreement?

What would the impact on effectiveness be when we transition from defining leadership to defining what it means to act in leadership and have a blueprint to make that determination?

The level of complexity significantly decreases due to the ability to eliminate hundreds, potentially, if not all, of the current leadership labels. We have an alternative, a highly effective method of defining what it means to be a leader. We have a solution that activates the third stage of the loop, decreasing complexity and increasing effectiveness.

The loop of optimal effectiveness helps us address complexity in all areas of our lives. Since this book is about the *Bible* and is associated with religion, it is essential to understand that the concept of complexity in relation to effectiveness is not unique to religion or churches. It impacts everything, including businesses, government, and our personal lives.

In the next chapter, we'll examine the complexity associated with the *Bible* and how most churches tend to operate. I am not picking on churches or organized religion. Most people are not aware of how complexity affects every part of our lives. I'm simply raising your level of awareness.

That brings us to the main purpose of this chapter. I am using the BASIC Leadership blueprint to illustrate how the *Bible* teaches acting in leadership. When a person uses any of the 1,000+ definitions of leadership to discuss the *Bible* in terms of leadership, the way the *Bible* passages and lessons are interpreted can be significantly different from how I present them in this book.

For instance, when we consider the premise that "in order to be a leader, a person must have followers," the language in the *Bible* can be misleading. Some translations use the word "followers." Jesus and his disciples are not a "leader, follower" structure. I will prove this in upcoming chapters.

Also, none of Jesus's teachings are based on positions in hierarchies, ethnicity, race, or gender. Do you think Jesus said, "OK, you're (insert race), so how you live life will be different?" Then he created a separate lesson based on that race? When we use any of the misguided leadership labels based on hierarchies, ethnicity, race, or gender, in my opinion, we are misinterpreting the lessons presented in the *Bible*.

The *Bible* teaches acting in leadership. It does not teach Hispanic, Black, White, Asian, Male, or Female designated leadership. The lessons of the *Bible* apply equally to everyone.

# CHAPTER THREE

# Foundational Principles & Universal Laws of Leadership

What do I mean by "foundational principles and universal laws?" Leadership is fundamentally about how we behave, how we act, and how we conduct ourselves. We see this "conduct" principle in the common language we use.

- The players conducted themselves impeccably, both on and off the field.
- She conducted herself as a professional and earned the respect of her coworkers.

Therefore, acting in leadership is based on how a person should behave, act, and conduct oneself.

There are foundational principles and universal laws that exist. They help us effectively and accurately evaluate the difference between moral and immoral behaviors.

Acting in leadership only happens when a person's thoughts, actions, progression, insight, and collaboration pass the integrity test and exist on the positive side of the leadership lifeline.

Therefore, we are talking about the qualities regarded as a characteristic or inherent part of someone or something that passes the integrity test and exists on the positive side of the leadership lifeline.

Examples are courage and honesty. These are attributes regarded as characteristics associated with leadership. The foundational principles and universal laws of how we should behave are the same for everyone.

Most of the over 1,000 modern-day labels and definitions "are not" derived from the foundational principles and universal laws of how we should live and behave. They include;

- ✓ Any label or definition created by attaching leadership to ethnicity, race, gender, age, or other identity-based characteristics.
- ✓ Any label or definition created by attaching leadership to a position in any hierarchy or associated with the functions of operating a business.

The foundational principles and universal laws that tell us murder, lying, stealing, and cheating are wrong;

those things do not change based on any ethnicity, race, gender, or other identity-based characteristics or the position a person holds in any hierarchy. They do not change whether you participate in business, government, politics, or non-profit entities.

Foundational principles and universal laws for moral behaviors are supported by science in two primary ways:

1. The release of the chemicals cortisol, adrenaline, oxytocin, serotonin, and dopamine. These built-in universal chemicals are activated based on our behaviors. It's a system that helps us define when we are acting in leadership.
2. The inherent, essential universal responses from our amygdala and hippocampus parts of our brain, which include guilt, shame, worry, anxiety, fear, love, joy, peace, and calm, are activated based on our behaviors. These built-in mechanisms help us define when we are acting in leadership.

As we work through each chapter, we will learn how these integral, hardwired mechanisms are activated.

Until I defined what it means to act in leadership under the BASIC Leadership blueprint, the misguided labels and definitions currently associated with leadership had overshadowed the foundational principles and universal laws that had been right in front of us the whole time.

The world is inundated with people who have written books, created podcasts, developed consulting companies, and given presentations on the concept of leadership. It has become a multi-billion-dollar industry.

According to Global Insight Services, the Leadership Development Program Market is anticipated to expand from $83.2 billion in 2024 to $218.9 billion by 2034.

Once a simple, lowly word, "Leadership" has become an industry of its own. So many people, names, and platforms are floating around in this industry that no one could possibly know them all.

The foundational principles and universal laws associated with what is now a full-blown industry called "Leadership" began under a multitude of other labels. The most recent label is Personal Development, which contains the foundational principles and universal laws that apply equally to everyone.

When the word "Leadership" was created and became part of our spoken language around 1809, we began our journey of replacing the foundational principles and universal laws of behavior with mystical, contradictory definitions and labels.

It's like the movie *Batman v Superman: Dawn of Justice*. Superman was once simple and good. Now, he's all muddled up, and we no longer understand what he represents. We have labels like "unethical leadership." Leaders are not unethical. There are unethical people. No one is coaching people to be unethical during their leadership coaching sessions. Why does that label even exist? We inherently know that being unethical is not a trait that Superman would possess. Something seems out of place.

The principle of non-contradiction, a cornerstone of logic, tells us that a statement and its negation cannot both be true at the same time and in the same sense; something cannot be both true and false simultaneously.

We cannot have the label of unethical leadership and then simultaneously teach that being unethical is not the trait of a leader. A person cannot be a leader and act unethically. By attaching leadership to a position in a hierarchy, we violate the principle of non-contradiction.

> *The principle of non-contradiction, a cornerstone of logic, tells us that a statement and its negation cannot both be true at the same time and in the same sense; something cannot be both true and false simultaneously.*

Let's work our way backwards in time. When we look at all the current platforms whose premise is built around the concept of leadership, they contain all of the "foundational principle and universal law" components that were once taught under the label of personal development.

The wording and language we use continue to expand over time. A slew of now readily available synonyms can be used to create what appear to be some new, unheard-of leadership principle. A synonym is a word or phrase that means exactly or nearly the same as another word or phrase in the same language.

Change Leadership and Transformational Leadership, two seemingly different things, are one and the same. Everything changes. The only constant is change. Therefore, there is no such thing as change leadership or transformational leadership. Everything and everyone transforms. These two misguided labels drive the level of complexity upward. People can create something new out of thin air because leadership has misguidedly been attached to a position in a hierarchy and associated with doing business.

In my book, *Back To BASIC: Acting In Leadership*, I take the readers on a journey back in time to the sources of the original foundational principles of acting in leadership. Those sources are the *Tao Te Ching*, the *Dhammapada*, Greek philosophy, and the *Bible*. The foundational principles and universal laws for how we should behave are the same for all four cultures in all four sources that existed thousands of miles apart and thousands of years ago.

This alignment does not mean that all four cultures agreed on everything or did not contradict one another in some areas. However, the foundational principles and universal laws for moral behaviors supported by science in two primary ways do not differ among the four sources. We find a very high level of consistency regarding moral and immoral behavior.

They didn't have some global summit where they hashed it all out, and then everyone went back to their homeland, where they wrote about societal behaviors. Most people never traveled more than five miles from where they were born, let alone thousands of miles.

As I wrote this chapter, I completed several searches to locate the names of leadership experts. Many people who launched different eras of personal development were not on those lists. This outcome is not unexpected. This result will always be the case with how things progress throughout history. The story would be the same if I asked you who the key players were in many major industries. If I asked you who the key players were who created the auto industry, you would probably include Henry Ford or Ford Motor Company.

You wouldn't even be close. Ford was a late-comer and failed at his first attempt to start a company. When Ford made his second attempt and established the Ford Motor Company, hundreds of automobile and truck manufacturers who had attempted to enter the auto industry or were still on the playing field existed. Ford is famous for automating the production line, allowing him to dominate the industry. That's the equivalent of someone entering the leadership industry around 2010, when the digital world came alive, and figuring out how to reach the top of the search engine results. They rose to the top quickly and achieved name recognition.

If you are a fan of John Maxwell, then you may already know this. He was a pastor who was writing books about leadership. All of the foundational principles he presents in his books are based on the foundational principles presented in the *Bible*. How do we know this? He has stated it publicly. His publisher told him that people in the business sector were purchasing the majority of his books and not in the religious sector. How do we know this? Yes, he has shared that story publicly as well.

So, Maxwell transitioned from creating materials for the religious sector to creating leadership books to help people in business. What did not change was that all the foundational fundamentals and principles in those books also came from the *Bible*.

First, we see one of the direct connections to how leadership becomes tied to the business world. That's where the demand was, so that's where Maxwell headed.

Second, if we look at the foundational principles, the fundamentals of his teachings, they apply to everything. We can take them out of the business realm and use them anywhere because they are not associated with any ethnicity, race, gender, or other identity-based characteristics or a position in any hierarchy.

Therefore, if a person implements many of the foundational principles taught by John Maxwell, they are, in fact, following the foundational principles of the *Bible*. People do not make this connection. They think it's just "leadership," and he's a "business leadership expert."

Once I have pointed this out to you, when you read any leadership book by any author, you can quickly separate the foundational principles from the leadership language that pertains to a position in a hierarchy, and is associated with operating a business.

When we go back in time, many of the most popular and influential people from the New Thought Movement of the late 1800s to the early 1900s, the Law of Attraction Movement from the early to mid-1900s, and the Personal Development Movement from the 1970s through the 1990s, all used the foundational principles and universal laws presented in the *Bible* to create their materials and platforms.

Dr. Wayne Dyer has written over 40 books; like Maxwell's, many are best sellers. Dyer says people should be Christ-like and Buddha-like rather than Christian or Buddhist. That's because being "Christ-like" addresses a person's behaviors. How we behave, how we act, how a person conducts oneself. The *Bible* tells us to look at our beliefs, our actions, how we progress in life, how we collaborate, and what we do with any insight we gain. It's asking us if we are acting with integrity and living on the positive side of the leadership lifeline.

The label "Christian" defines a group of people. It's a religious group identifier, like Lutheran or Catholic. This group identity approach is an excellent example of how we are led astray when we create leadership labels based on identity characteristics such as ethnicity, race, gender, age, or position in a hierarchy. Acting in leadership is the same for Christians as it is for Buddhists. Dyer uses the foundational principles from the *Tao Te Ching* by Buddha and the *Bible*.

In his book, *How to Win Friends and Influence People*, Dale Carnegie tells us where he got all his foundational principles. He lists Jesus as one of the people.

Everyone gets their ideas from somewhere. Sure, people think up new things. I created the loop of optimal effectiveness and the BASIC™ Leadership blueprint. However, the foundational principles of life are the same for everyone and have been around for thousands of years. Acting in leadership is based on the foundational principles and universal laws of life.

> *You've got to be a little suspicious of someone who says, 'I've got a new fundamental.' That's like someone inviting you to tour a factory where they are manufacturing antiques.* ~Jim Rohn

If a person practices the foundational principles taught in leadership platforms, they are, in fact, following the foundational principles of the *Bible*. People do not realize this direct connection. They think it's just "leadership," something new and revolutionary.

If you have been hesitant to read the *Bible* or, for some reason, have an aversion to religion, you shouldn't. The foundational principles of the new thought movement, the law of attraction movement, the personal development movement, or the current-day leadership lessons are all derived from the teachings of the Bible.

# CHAPTER FOUR

# What Is The *Bible*?

When we are young, we do not begin learning math by starting with algebra or trigonometry. We learn 1 + 1 = 2. When we learn a language, we do not start by trying to understand adverbs or adjectives. We begin with simple words, such as Cat, Dog, and Tree, while pointing to a picture of them. We need to use this same strategy when it comes to the *Bible*.

I made some statements in chapter two and want to make sure you haven't forgotten. The concept of complexity in relation to effectiveness is not unique to the *Bible*, religion, or churches. It impacts everything, including businesses, government, and our personal lives. In this chapter, I am not picking on churches or organized religion. I'm addressing complexity. Most people are not aware of how complexity affects every part of our lives. It's simply a matter of awareness.

As you already learned in the introduction of this book, religion wasn't a great experience for me in my youth. Because of my upbringing, all my life, I had looked at the *Bible* as a moral 2 x 4 that *Bible*-thumpers carried around to hit people on the head and let others know they are sinners and all going to hell. It was a way that others illustrated some sort of moral superiority. My mindset was, "Hey, look at goody-two-shoes over there." The *Bible* was something missionaries took with them to impoverished countries. It was the giant book that pastors and preachers used to give sermons. That's all I ever knew about the *Bible* from my viewpoint.

When I began to reengage with the church, the sermons and messages presented at churches were like starting with algebra when I did not understand the 1 + 1 = 2 of the *Bible*. The loop of optimal effectiveness was in full play. I got what felt like calculus math and a moral thumping over the head. It was like being in kindergarten, and I was supposed to know what acquiescence meant. Then, it always ended with being asked to hand over some of my hard-earned cash. I felt like the school bully just beat me up, and his reward was my lunch money.

Ever hear the term, "You're preaching to the choir?" You see, the choir consists of people who already go to church; most already understand the basics. They are at the algebraic or calculus level of religion. Most pastors and preachers preach to the choir, then wonder why there's not a stampede of people running to churches or their sermons. It's not intentional.

How do we fix this issue? Let's start with the basics, as we do in math, with $1 + 1 = 2$. If you asked people, "What is the *Bible*?" What kind of responses would you get? I believe that just like asking a person, "What is leadership?" the answers would be all over the place. We have to begin with the fundamentals.

The *Bible*;

- Consists of 66 different books all combined into one. It's a library of books.
- Was originally written in three different languages, Hebrew, Aramaic, and Greek, across three different continents.
- The 66 books were written over a 1,500-year period.
- The collection was written by 40 different authors, including shepherds, farmers, fishermen, priests, philosophers, doctors, and kings.
- There are multiple translations into English, using different translations of words.
- Fewer word choices existed when it was written, but our vocabulary is more extensive now. The authors chose what they thought were the best or most accurate words.
- It's a collection of stories, poems, prophecies, letters, laws, histories, and biographies written by people.
- Most people did not read or write when the books of the *Bible* were written. Therefore,

many of the lessons are told through parables, metaphors, and analogies, with some written in rhythmic or poetic verse. These types of writing help people remember so they can pass the lessons on to others.

- Some lessons are presented in very simple ways, and some in very complex ways.
- All the individual books of the *Bible* contain all the foundational principles of acting in leadership that we clammer after today.

That's quite different than how I viewed the *Bible* in my youth. If someone had started with those ten bullet points, told me that the *Bible* is full of crazy and insane stories mirroring modern-day scripts from sci-fi, action, or drama movies, that it had some poetic verses, biographies, life lessons of leadership we learn today about money, health, relationships, and personal development, then asked if I thought that was pretty cool, I would have said, "Holy crap. That's crazy." Then, if they followed up by asking me if I wanted to know more, I would have said, "Heck yeah."

If people knew simple things like who wrote each book, to whom it was written, and why it was written, and how it all relates to acting in leadership, how many people do you think might be interested in learning more? Remember that "leadership" is one of the most consistently searched terms on the internet.

Go out and ask people, "What is the *Bible*?" See what kind of responses you get. Ask anyone, including people who regularly attend church. Ask a few pastors, too. Then, when they ask you that same question, give some form of this response. You do not have to memorize it; make your own interesting version.

> *It's a collection of 66 books written over 1,500 years across three continents by 40 different authors, including shepherds, fishermen, priests, and kings. It contains exciting stories like modern-day sci-fi, action, and drama movie scripts. It contains poems, biographies, laws, and personal letters, all illustrating the lessons of modern-day leadership principles. Nothing like it exists anywhere else.*

What do you think about this distinctly different approach to introducing people to the *Bible*? How about you? Do you want to know more? Excellent, keep reading.

Those ten bullet points open our eyes and help us to begin to understand the basics of the *Bible*. Let's look at the 66 books in the order they appear in the *Bible*. I created this list using The New International Version (NIV), published by Zondervan. We will also use this as an example to demonstrate how the loop of optimal effectiveness works. We will increase the complexity level by adding the author's name most often attributed to each book.

1. Genesis (Moses)
2. Exodus (Moses)
3. Leviticus (Moses)
4. Numbers (Moses)
5. Deuteronomy (Moses)

6. Joshua (Joshua)
7. Judges (Samuel)
8. Ruth (Samuel)
9. 1 Samuel (Samuel, Nathan, and Gad)
10. 2 Samuel (Samuel, Nathan, and Gad)
11. 1 Kings (Jeremiah)
12. 2 Kings (Jeremiah)
13. 1 Chronicles (Erza)
14. 2 Chronicles (Erza)
15. Ezra (Erza)
16. Nehemiah (Nehemiah)
17. Esther (Esra or Nehemiah)
18. Job (Job)
19. Psalms (King David, Asaph, Son of Korah, King Solomon, Ethan, Heman)
20. Proverbs (King Solomon)
21. Ecclesiastes (King Solomon)
22. Song of Songs (King Solomon)
23. Isaiah (Isaiah) 16
24. Jeremiah (Jeremiah)
25. Lamentations (Jeremiah)
26. Ezekiel (Ezekiel)
27. Daniel (Daniel)
28. Hosea (Hosea)
29. Joel (Joel)
30. Amos (Amos)
31. Obadiah (Obadiah)
32. Jonah (Jonah)
33. Micah (Micah)
34. Nahum (Nahum)

35. Habakkuk (Habakkuk)
36. Zephaniah (Zephaniah)
37. Haggai (Haggai)
38. Zechariah (Zechariah)
39. Malachi (Malachi)

That list is from the Old Testament. It includes 39 books and 30 authors, some of whom are attributed to more than one book. How are we doing so far regarding the complexity level? Let's continue by adding the books of the New Testament.

40. Matthew (Matthew)
41. Mark (John Mark)
42. Luke (Luke)
43. John (John)
44. Acts of the Apostles (Luke)
45. Romans (Paul)
46. 1 Corinthians (Paul)
47. 2 Corinthians (Paul)
48. Galatians (Paul)
49. Ephesians (Paul)
50. Philippians (Paul)
51. Colossians (Paul, Timothy)
52. 1 Thessalonians (Paul)
53. 2 Thessalonians (Paul)
54. 1 Timothy (Paul)
55. 2 Timothy (Paul)
56. Titus (Paul)
57. Philemon (Paul)

58. Hebrews (Paul)
59. James (James, half-brother of Jesus)
60. 1 Peter (Peter)
61. 2 Peter (Peter)
62. 1 John (John)
63. 2 John (John)
64. 3 John (John)
65. Jude (Jude, half-brother of Jesus)
66. Revelation (John)

Again, you do not have to memorize this list or do anything with it. We're gaining insight into how levels of complexity impact effectiveness. Let's say your goal is to introduce more people to the *Bible* because the *Bible* teaches acting in Leadership. How effective would you be if the level of complexity is high? How high would the complexity appear if someone didn't understand the basics?

Complexity regarding the *Bible* is created in other ways as well. Books 40 through 44, Matthew through Acts, are called "The Gospels." The word "Gospel" means "news". Books 45 through 65, Romans through Jude, are called "The epistles." An epistle is a "Letter." Next, an Apostle is a "messenger."

Let's put this in current-day language. Some people wrote the news, and others wrote letters. They were messengers who brought that news and those letters to others.

However, spreading news and reading letters is not the language we hear in most churches or from people attempting to introduce people to the *Bible*.

You're sitting in church for the first time, and the paster begins with, "According to the Apostle Paul in his epistle, 2 Corinthians 9:6, "Remember this: Whoever sows sparingly will also reap sparingly, and whoever sows generously will also reap generously."

What is an Apostle? Who is Paul? What is an epistle? What the heck does 2 Corinthians 9:6 mean? It's not that any pastor does this intentionally to look intelligent or superior. I think they miss the point that most people aren't *Bible* or religious scholars who know what any of these labels and words mean. Second, most people, including pastors, are not familiar with the concept of complexity and effectiveness. People need $1 + 1 = 2$ first.

Many things can detract people from the primary purposes of the *Bible*. One purpose is to teach us the lessons of acting in leadership. When people go down into some bottomless abyss, having debates about who wrote what and when, what does that do to the effectiveness of learning the lessons? You are correct; it raises the level of complexity. Complexity leads to people being disengaged. The lessons of acting in leadership, as taught in the *Bible*, are simple. For many people, the *Bible* itself can appear very complex. It is not.

We will continue to address complexity as we learn how the *Bible* teaches the lessons of acting in leadership.

# CHAPTER FIVE

# Parables, Analogies, and Metaphors

A man named Jonah became aware of how the city of Nineveh had grown into a dumpster fire in terms of any sense of morality. Think of this city as a constant, never-ending spring break party in Miami Beach, Florida—a giant hedonistic celebration.

Jonah's conscience tells him he should go to Nineveh to help. He should explain to the Ninevites why their behaviors are undesirable and that there will be consequences if they do not address this mess. However, Jonah faces some challenges.

Jonah was a real person who lived in Gath-Hepher, a border town in the Northern Kingdom of Israel. Nineveh was the capital of Assyria, a brutal empire that threatened the northern kingdom of Israel. Jonah would be walking into potentially hostile territory, and it would take him three days to reach it. He couldn't just jump in a car and take a quick road trip.

The city had around 120,000 people, which was a massive city for those times. Jonah was a regular Joe-schmoe like you and me. He did not hold any position of authority. He'd have to stroll on in all by himself and begin pointing out the issues and the consequences of their behaviors.

I used spring break in Miami, Florida, as an analogy. What was happening in the city of Nineveh makes spring break look mild by comparison. You and I might volunteer to go to spring break somewhere and talk to some kids, but I doubt that you or I would have gone to Nineveh in those times. The Ninevites constantly tortured men, raped women, and killed children. Nineveh was a really, really horrible place. It's a dumpster fire inside a train wreck inside a hurricane.

Jonah does what any sane person would do: He weighs his options. One option is to do nothing. He thinks to himself, "Yeah, I'm not going to do that. That's a long walk and probably not going to end well for me." And that is the option he acts on rather than the second option, which is to do something about it.

Jonah's conscience nags at him so strongly that he jumps on a boat to avoid this seemingly impossible task. He is hiding from his conscience. It's the equivalent of the Miami Beach police department saying, "We're not going to do anything about all of this destruction and naughty behavior. Let those kids wreck crap and terrorize the other residents. Let's all leave the city instead. Then, we won't have to put ourselves at risk. It's someone else's problem, not ours."

So Jonah gets on a boat and heads out to sea. The sea turns rough, and the boat is in danger. Except it's not just him on the boat. There are others on the boat in harm's way from the storm. Now, they are trying to figure out if someone knew about this storm and didn't do anything about it. "Hey, did anyone have access to a weather app on their smartphone? You saw this storm coming but didn't tell us?"

Jonah tells the others on the boat, "Yeah, I knew." He knew about the storm and didn't do anything. It was not their first choice, but the others on the boat eventually threw Jonah into the sea. Instead of drowning, a large fish comes from the ocean's depths and swallows him whole. He's in the belly of this giant beast for three days, and then he gets spit out directly onto the land.

That could have taken a different twist since fish have two exits. A good book always has a poop joke.

After three days of agony from bathing in an acidic tomb of the giant fish's stomach, Jonah changes his mind. He regains his ethical bearings, musters up the courage, and decides to go to Nineveh to bring the lessons of the *Bible* to the people. In due course, his messages reach the King. The people begin to change their ways, saving the city from its morally decaying destruction. The story of Jonah is a parable.

## *Parables, Analogies, and Metaphors*

A parable is a simple story illustrating a moral or spiritual lesson. An analogy is a comparison between two things, typically for the purpose of explanation or clarification. I used spring break activities in Miami Beach, Florida, as a way to describe what the city of Nineveh would be like. That's an analogy. A metaphor is a thing regarded as representative or symbolic of something else, especially something abstract like guilt. In this story, guilt is illustrated as the equivalent of three days in the stomach acid of a sea monster.

The *Bible* is filled with parables, analogies, and metaphors. The Book of Matthew, chapter 13, verses 34 to 35, tells us this is the case.

> *Jesus spoke all these things to the crowd in parables; he did not say anything to them without using a parable. So was fulfilled what was spoken through the prophet:*
>
> *"I will open my mouth in parables,*
>
> *I will utter things hidden since the creation of the world."*
> ~Matthew 13:34-35 (NIV)

That's right, the story of Jonah and the Whale is a parable. Parables can consist of actual events, places, people, and actions taken or not taken. Parables can also contain fictitious components.

My wife Lisa and I love to watch nature shows. A person would have a very difficult time convincing me that any species of large fish or sea monster, if one existed, including a whale, could swallow a person whole. Then that person lived for three days in its belly, and then the sea monster barfed that person up onto the shoreline alive.

Could a person be swallowed by a large fish and live in its belly for three days, then get vomited up by that fish and still be alive? One person might say, "Of course not. That's just silly." Another might say, "Oh yes. That actually happened." Both arguments are based on beliefs.

We could also ask if Jonah actually got on a boat or if it was simply a metaphor. We can certainly speculate. We're not here to debate the "really happened or didn't actually happen" aspects of the story. We're here to learn how the *Bible* teaches acting in leadership. This parable teaches a multitude of modern-day lessons associated with acting in leadership.

What we do know is that Jonah was a real person, and the city of Nineveh was a real place. Nineveh was becoming a giant version of a never-ending spring break party, and no one was doing anything about it. Nineveh was a dumpster fire inside a train wreck inside a hurricane. Jonah knew about it; he knew the solution, and eventually, he went there to do something about it.

Let's look at what we can learn from this parable.

✓ When a fire occurs, we know we must do our best to put it out, or it will spread and burn more things. This inevitable damage is also true of destructive behaviors. If cities like

Miami Beach did nothing about drunkenness, destruction of private property, and inappropriate sexual conduct during spring break, we know what would happen. It would spread. More people would show up in Miami Beach next year, and the levels of destruction and lewd behavior would escalate.

✓ Our conscience is an inner feeling or voice that guides the rightness or wrongness of one's behavior. When we do not act in accordance with what our conscience tells us, we suffer. That's the power of guilt at work. Three days in the stomach of a giant fish, taking an acidic bath is akin to the feeling we get in our gut when we do not act, then we feel guilty. It's a three-day acid guilt bath. His guilt ate him up so badly for three days that he decided to do something about it, regardless of the risk to himself. When a person comes to their senses, they go from an uncertain, wavy sea to having balance on firm ground.

✓ Jonah took responsibility and was willing to suffer the consequences.

✓ When they followed Jonah's advice to punish him by tossing him into the sea, it didn't alleviate their own guilt. They were still stricken with fear because what they did had not solved the actual problems in Nineveh.

✓ The boat they were in represents their own city. The storm rages, the fire is burning in

Nineveh, and the flames of destruction are headed their way. Remember, when fire and behaviors go unchecked, they eventually spread your way. We can deduce that the boat is simply a metaphor for the city where Jonah lived.

✓ Jonah was not a king, nor did he hold any other top-level position in society. Just like you and me, he was an average Joe. It is up to everyone to act in leadership and do the right thing. It is not anyone else's responsibility. And most certainly not anyone else's responsibility because they hold a higher position in any hierarchy.

There are multiple lessons in all the stories of the *Bible.* People see them as some hallucinogenic, unrealistic story from the Bronze Age. The writers told stories to depict how things get corrupted and how things like the suffering that will happen when you don't act rightly.

The state gets corrupted. You're called upon to tell your fellow man or enemy when they behave poorly. When your conscience tells you to do that, and you don't, the whole ship will start to rock. The storm will head your way if you do nothing.

During the holocaust, Martin Niemöller was a prominent Lutheran pastor in Germany in the 1940s. As Jews and others were rounded up and taken to concentration camps, most people did nothing.

> *First they came for the socialists, and I did not speak out because I was not a socialist.*
> *Then they came for the trade unionists, and I did not speak out because I was not a trade unionist.*
> *Then they came for the Jews, and I did not speak out because I was not a Jew.*
> *Then they came for me, and there was no one left to speak for me.*
> ~Martin Niemöller

Pastor Niemöller's quote paints a vivid picture of what happens when we do nothing to stand up against evil. They made a movie about how Pastor Niemöller stood up against these horrific behaviors. This same lesson is taught in the *Bible* through the Book of Jonah. It's done through the experiences of those times and presented using the language of those times. Pastor Niemöller and the events of the holocaust were real. So was Jonah and his actions to change the culture of an entire city. Both stories teach us the same lesson.

These are powerful images that stick with us. A tossing ship. Swallowed by a giant fish. Bathing in stomach acid. Being taken down into the black abyss of the ocean. An image we relate to what the pits of hell might be like. Guilt gives us that "living in the pits of hell" feeling.

Most people don't sit around after a movie and discuss what the movie meant. They just enjoy it. But that doesn't mean they didn't learn anything from it.

They just don't reflect on what they learned. This lack of reflection has changed. There are forums on the internet where people discuss the themes and lessons of movies. We could label them Movie Study Groups. "Hey, everyone, I'll catch up with you later. I'm off to Movie Study Group."

Why do people make fun of things like *Bible* study groups? The point of *Bible* Study is to reflect on what you've learned. A *Bible* study would be no different than a book club where you discuss the book. There are forums now where people meet to discuss the lessons of leadership. Guess what? The foundational principles and the fundamentals of leadership lessons originated in the *Bible*.

# CHAPTER SIX

# Lessons Of Acting In Leadership

We learned in chapter four that the *Bible* is a library of 66 books written by at least 40 distinctly different people, such as shepherds, farmers, fishermen, priests, philosophers, doctors, and kings. This library of books took 1,500 years to accumulate. It is a collection of stories, poems, prophecies, letters, laws, histories, and biographies. Within all of those different writings are the lessons of acting in leadership. The authors present those lessons using parables, metaphors, analogies, and poetic and song lyrics style verses. Since a large portion of the population did not read or write, these types of writing styles help people remember the lessons.

In the list of books from chapter four, the 40th book is called The Book of Matthew. Matthew was one of the original twelve disciples of Jesus. Disciple means student. To disciple someone means to teach them. Jesus was the Teacher, and Matthew was the student. Matthew was not following Jesus. Jesus was teaching his students to follow the lessons he taught. Jesus said, "Join me." Some translations use the word "follow." We don't follow groups or clubs; we join them. Of course, this misguided concept about followers is being reinforced because we use the language of "following someone" on social media platforms.

Each book of the *Bible* is made up of chapters. This structure would be like any book you have today. The book has a title and chapters—chapter 1, chapter 2, etc. The only difference is that the *Bible* assigns a number to each sentence or group of sentences. This number assignment allows a person to quickly locate chapters and sentences with pinpoint accuracy. Instead of calling them sentences, they are referred to as verses. We refer to the lines of poems as verses. It's the same thing.

Book, chapter, and verse. Once you understand the breakdown, there is no complexity. In fact, the complexity level has been reduced regarding our ability to locate things quickly. When I search for something in modern-day books, it isn't easy to locate a specific line within that book unless it is an eBook with a search function. Then, it's a bit faster. The structure of the *Bible* provides a high level of effectiveness for locating any specific verse. The loop of optimal effectiveness is at play here.

## Some Lessons Of Acting In Leadership

Earlier, we discussed how important it is to know who wrote the book, why they wrote it, to whom it was written, and the lessons within. When we read anything, including modern-day literature, and we have this information, we also get context.

> *Context is the circumstances that form the setting for an event, statement, or idea, and in which it can be fully understood and assessed.*

We'll begin with the Book of Matthew, chapters 5 through 7. Chapters 5 through 7 pertain to the Sermon on the Mount, a presentation that Jesus gave to a crowd outside on a large hill. A sermon is a presentation, hence the name. It's the 2,000-year-old version of a modern-day TED Talk.

Jesus gave a TED Talk, and Matthew wrote it down. It took place on a big hill outside in front of a large group of people. As with most TED Talks, this one contained a whole bunch of lessons: lessons about how we behave, how we act, how a person conducts oneself; the lessons about acting in leadership.

Ok, that's a pretty darn cool image right there. People flocked to this TED Talk from miles and miles away, not unlike people who sought out the seminars of Dale Carnegie in the 1930s. Carnegie's book, *How To Win Friends & Influence People*, was published in 1936. Carnegie's seminars happened during the great depression, and people came from miles around to learn from him. If Carnegie had given one of his presentations two thousand years ago on a large hill outside, it might have been called The Sermon on the Mount.

If you asked anyone who teaches leadership about whether the little acts we do in life matter, what would they tell you? They would tell you that the little things matter. Let's see how modern-day teachings match the lessons taught in the Sermon on the Mount.

*Murder*

> *You have heard that it was said to the people long ago, "You shall not murder, and anyone who murders will be subject to judgment." But I tell you that anyone who is angry with a brother or sister will be subject to judgment. Again, anyone who says to a brother or sister, "Raca," is answerable to the court. And anyone who says, "You fool!" will be in danger of the fire of hell.*
> ~Matthew 5:21-22 (NIV)

Note how the location within the *Bible* is referenced at the end of the quote. When you know what those numbers and letters mean, that passage is easy to locate, right? The Book of Matthew, chapter 5, verses 21 to 22. It also tells us which translation of the *Bible* I used. NIV is the New International Version.

Lesson: Little things matter. We tend to view anger as a little thing. It is not. The *Bible* tells us that harboring anger towards someone is the moral equivalent of murder. Why? Because anger can lead to murder. We tend to live our lives by ranking things based on a perceived level of evil and how bad they seem. We think, "Anger isn't as bad as murder, so it's no big deal." We view murder as horrific; then we use that as our base comparison to justify that somehow anger isn't so bad.

Anger can be a stepping stone to murder. In fact, many murders are committed out of rage. This passage is a representation, an analogy, that teaches us two things.

1. We need to view anger as bad as murder
2. We need to view it that way because the little things we deem as less critical can lead to horrible things. Little leads to big.

Modern-day leadership lessons include lessons about how the little things matter as much as the big things. I'll just do a little bit of cocaine, not a lot, so don't worry. I only took some staples from work, not a stapler, so it's okay. Those little things aren't really that bad. I just get angry once in a while. It's not like I'm always angry, so I don't have to worry.

Viewing anger as less critical than murder is like a person who is 150 pounds overweight saying, "Well, I'm not as bad as that person over there who is 250 pounds overweight, so I don't need to take my health situation seriously. Then, one day, you're 250 pounds overweight, and you have a heart attack or stroke.

We do the same thing with finances. "Hey, I don't spend as foolishly as that person over there. I only have

$7,000 in credit card debt. They have $20,000 in credit card debt. Glad I'm not them." Then, we continue to accumulate debt little by little until we have to file for bankruptcy.

Murder, becoming unhealthy, and going into debt all begin as little things. They can grow to a level that destroys our lives. In the Sermon on the Mount, Jesus gets very specific about how "little turns into big."

### The Parables of the Mustard Seed and the Yeast

> He told them another parable: "The kingdom of heaven is like a mustard seed, which a man took and planted in his field. Though it is the smallest of all seeds, yet when it grows, it is the largest of garden plants and becomes a tree, so that the birds come and perch in its branches."
> ~Matthew 13:31-32 (NIV)

Little things lead to big things, whether we act with or without integrity or on the positive or negative side of the leadership lifeline. Little acts of badness can grow into big acts of badness, and little acts of goodness can grow into large acts of goodness.

We can no longer use excuses like, "Oh, it's just a little lie. It's not that big of a deal." A mustard seed can grow into a big tree of lies. Today we use the analogy "a web of lies." We spin enough lies and eventually get caught in our own web.

Let's go a bit deeper. If you asked anyone who teaches leadership, what would those coaches tell you about hypocrisy? They would say that being a hypocrite is also not an attribute of a leader.

What did Jesus say about hypocrisy in his TED Talk, The Sermon on the Mount? The Book of Matthew, chapter 7, verses 1 to 5, tells us.

### Judging Others

*Do not judge, or you too will be judged. For in the same way you judge others, you will be judged, and with the measure you use, it will be measured to you.*

*Why do you look at the speck of sawdust in your brother's eye and pay no attention to the plank in your own eye? How can you say to your brother, "Let me take the speck out of your eye," when all the time there is a plank in your own eye? You hypocrite, first take the plank out of your own eye, and then you will see clearly to remove the speck from your brother's eye.*
~Matthew 7:1-5 (NIV)

Look at the wording and presentation of this lesson. Jesus uses analogies and metaphors with colorful language. A spec of sawdust and a plank of wood in a person's eye conjures up images that are glued into our memory.

There are multiple lessons, one about hypocrisy and one about judging others. Judging others for things you do yourself makes you a hypocrite. It also tells us of the remedy. Fix yourself first; then, you've earned the right to offer advice to others. To provide guidance, to say the truth. The *Bible* does not tell us not to judge; throughout the various books, it tells us how to judge.

We make judgments all day long. They are essential. Judgment is the ability to make considered decisions or come to sensible conclusions. The Book of Ephesians, chapter 4, verse 29, helps us to define the type of guidance and truth we provide to others.

> *Do not let any unwholesome talk come out of your mouths, but only what is helpful for building others up according to their needs, that it may benefit those who listen.*
> ~ Ephesians 4:29 (NIV)

Examples of some things you do yourself that make you a hypocrite are addressed in chapters five and six of the Book of Matthew. Those chapters reference murder, adultery, revenge, hate, greed, and worry, to name a few. You judge others while doing the things you're calling out another person for doing. You lied the other day, and now you're judging or calling out another person for lying. You hypocrite.

In the Book of John, chapter 8, verses 2 to 9, we see the lessons about judgment and hypocrisy play out in real time.

*At dawn he appeared again in the temple courts,
where all the people gathered around him, and he sat
down to teach them. The teachers of the law and the
Pharisees brought in a woman caught in adultery.
They made her stand before the group and said to
Jesus, "Teacher, this woman was caught in the act of
adultery. In the Law Moses commanded us to stone
such women. Now what do you say?" They were
using this question as a trap, in order to have a basis
for accusing him.*

*But Jesus bent down and started to write on the
ground with his finger. When they kept on
questioning him, he straightened up and said to
them, "Let any one of you who is without sin be the
first to throw a stone at her." Again he stooped down
and wrote on the ground.*

*At this, those who heard began to go away one at a
time, the older ones first, until only Jesus was left,
with the woman still standing there.*
~John 8:2-9 (NIV)

Everyone who was judging her was guilty of acting
immorally at some point in their life. They all knew that
if stoning her was the answer, they should all get in line
for a good rock pummeling. They all walked away.

We have context, the circumstances that form the setting for an event, statement, or idea, and in terms of which it can be fully understood and assessed.

Throughout this book, I have attempted to provide context so that what I present can be fully understood and assessed. You have been gaining insight.

*Insight is the capacity to gain an accurate and deep intuitive understanding.*

Understanding the *Bible* so a person can learn the lessons of acting in leadership is a worthy ideal. We have been collaborating through this book. The actions you take or do not take will be a direct result of your beliefs because of what you have read. You will progress toward something, good or bad. We are always progressing toward something and moving forward in life, whether we participate or not in controlling that trajectory.

During this progression, when you act with integrity and on the positive side of the leadership lifeline, you have been acting in leadership and, thereby, a leader.

Acting with integrity and on the positive side of the leadership lifeline is how we impact the trajectory of our lives. So many people tell us we have the ability to impact the trajectory of our lives, yet they cannot provide a simple, non-complex blueprint for doing so. The BASIC Leadership blueprint is simple and effective.

We are all hypocrites at some point. Does anyone instantly stop being one? No. It's a progression. We know it's a progression because Matthew 7:24 provides that insight. It tells us that we must continually "practice" just as one practices anything to become good at it and make it a habit.

> *Therefore everyone who hears these words of mine and puts them into practice is like a wise man who built his house on the rock. The rain came down, the streams rose, and the winds blew and beat against that house; yet it did not fall, because it had its foundation on the rock.*
> ~Matthew 7:24-25 (NIV)

To not be a hypocrite is a worthy ideal. It's a progression that takes practice. You must believe that it is possible. See how the BASIC Leadership blueprint works? Hypocrisy is a good example for illustrating the connection between the components of belief, action, success, insight, collaboration, integrity, and the leadership lifeline. Being a hypocrite is not an attribute of a leader.

The attributes of acting in leadership include the small things some people consider insignificant. They are just as important as the big things like murder.

Once you understand the basics of the *Bible*, what seems like complexity disappears. Once you understand how the BASIC Leadership blueprint works, the complexity associated with what makes a person a leader disappears. And once we see the connection between the lessons of acting in leadership and the *Bible*, we are more likely to be drawn to it.

We start with $1 + 1 = 2$ and move on to $2 + 2 = 4$. We progress from easy and simple to slightly more complex. Let's continue.

# CHAPTER SEVEN

# More Lessons

I began my career in the business world in the 1980s. This decade was part of the personal development movement. There was no internet, no cell phones, and the concept of online or video seminars had not yet taken place. People attended seminars in person, and boy, oh boy, did they.

Salespeople and corporate executives flocked to see the personal development gurus of the 1980s. Zig Ziglar, Brian Tracy, and Jim Rohn were some of the most sought-after.

We learned how John Maxwell transitioned from writing his books for the religious sector to directing them in the business world. Like Maxwell, who put his focus on executives of the business world during the 1980s and 90s, the personal development movement focused heavily on helping sales teams. You could purchase cassette tapes and training packets by the boatload. I was in sales during this period and had personally been to seminars by both Ziglar and Tracy.

If you've ever been in sales, the training of the top-producing companies and teams includes a focus on staying positive, creating a certain mindset for success, handling rejection, and deflecting negativity.

If you were in sales before the Internet, sales were done primarily by phone or in person. I visited a lot of companies. The number of motivational posters plastered all over corporate walls was incredible. I walked down some hallways with ten or twenty nicely framed pictures of sunsets, rainbows, adorable animals, and rivers embedded with motivational phrases displayed in large, bold fonts. Many companies would spend big dollars to put fancy art on walls, giving the impression that "we're successful." Placing motivational posters on corporate walls gave the impression that "we inspire and uplift, we encourage positive attitudes, and boost morale."

Another name for the phrases on these posters is "proverb." A proverb is a short, concise, and forcefully expressive saying that is in general use. It provides a universal truth or piece of sound advice. Many of the proverbs I saw then, and still see today, come from within every Book of the *Bible*. In fact, one of the books of the *Bible* is named Proverbs.

The Book of Proverbs has 31 chapters and 915 verses. That's quite the collection for that time or at any time. If you are already inclined to be drawn to motivational posters and the lessons they provide, then you will love the Book of Proverbs.

We get more context when we combine a bunch of short, concise phrases that offer a universal truth or sound advice. That's the Book of Proverbs: a compilation of universal truths and pieces of sound advice with context. All of the concepts presented on those motivational posters exist in the *Bible*. Now, they exist in abundance on social media platforms such as Instagram.

The Book of Proverbs is generally attributed to King Solomon. We learned that books of the *Bible* were written by people who held a wide variety of social positions. These include fishermen, shepherds, farmers, philosophers, priests, and kings. Proverbs was written by a King.

We have the blueprint for defining what it means to act in leadership. Acting in leadership is about all parts of our lives, including our physical and mental health, finances, and relationships.

The Book of Proverbs, chapter 3, verses 1 and 2, tells us that acting in leadership will prolong our lives and bring us peace and prosperity.

*Wisdom Bestows Well-Being*

> *My son, do not forget my teaching,*
> *but keep my commands in your heart,*
> *for they will prolong your life many years*
> *and bring you peace and prosperity*
> ~Proverbs 3:1-2 (NIV)

How do we prolong our lives and have peace of mind? We prolong our lives by eating healthier and getting exercise. Our lives are also extended when we reduce or remove stress and anxiety. Reducing anxiety and stress creates peace of mind.

Today, we have the science that tells us what stress and anxiety do to our bodies and the impact on our longevity, as well as the things we do to cause most of that stress. They did not have that exact science, yet knew what we know today. That's called wisdom and insight. The first chapter, lines 1 through 7, tells us the purpose of the Book of Proverbs.

*The proverbs of Solomon son of David, king of Israel:*

> *for gaining wisdom and instruction;*
> *for understanding words of insight;*
> *for receiving instruction in prudent behavior,*
> *doing what is right and just and fair;*
> *for giving prudence to those who are simple,*
> *knowledge and discretion to the young—*
> *let the wise listen and add to their learning,*
> *and let the discerning get guidance—*
> *for understanding proverbs and parables,*
> *the sayings and riddles of the wise.*
> *The fear of the Lord is the beginning of knowledge,*
> *but fools despise wisdom and instruction.*
> ~Proverbs 1:1-7 (NIV)

So, what is the purpose of the Book of Proverbs?

- ✓ To gain wisdom and insight.
- ✓ To gain knowledge on prudent behavior.
- ✓ To do what is right and just and fair.

✓ To act with integrity and on the positive side of the leadership lifeline.
✓ To share this wisdom with others.
✓ And how to interpret the lessons hidden within parables, the riddles of the wise.

"WOW!" is the only response that comes to mind.

The first chapter of Proverbs discusses not hanging out with people who sin. Let's clarify what sinning means. We think in terms of committing murder, stealing, etc. Again, we miss how it pertains to what we tend to see as small, insignificant things.

The *Bible* discusses sins such as gluttony, treating people poorly, and having a bad attitude. It even addresses the effects of having negative or positive thoughts. When a person's mind is consumed with negative thoughts, it's almost impossible to have a positive life.

> *For though we live in the world, we do not wage war as the world does. The weapons we fight with are not the weapons of the world. On the contrary, they have divine power to demolish strongholds. We demolish arguments and every pretension that sets itself up against the knowledge of God, and we take captive every thought to make it obedient to Christ.*
> ~2 Corinthians 10:3-5 (NIV)

The phrase "The weapons we fight with are not the weapons of the world" refers to controlling our attitude, mindset, and beliefs. How do we know this? It tells us, "we take captive every thought."

Our actions are obedient to our thoughts. Our beliefs drive our actions. Our thoughts have a stronghold on the trajectory of our lives. Our thoughts determine how we progress and in what direction. When a person's mind is consumed with negative thoughts, it's almost impossible to have a positive life. The stronghold is our negative thoughts.

Our thoughts, health, and finances are all addressed in the *Bible*. Eat like crap, become obese, and your life will be shortened. Living in worry all the time and having high levels of anxiety will release chemicals like cortisol and adrenaline into your body, which damages your cells, leading to a shorter life. In highly developed countries, what we refer to as first-world countries, obesity and stress are two of the top silent killers.

These chemicals provide the "science" behind the foundational principles and universal laws we referred to in chapter three. It wasn't until the twentieth century (1900s) that we fully understood the science behind the chemicals of cortisol, adrenaline, oxytocin, serotonin, and dopamine. These chemicals play a huge role in determining when a person acts in leadership. They are punishment and reward chemicals attached to specific behaviors. We'll start with cortisol and adrenaline.

Cortisol can affect our bodies in both positive and negative ways. On the positive side, it helps the body respond to stress or danger, preparing it for fight-or-flight situations; it helps with metabolism, immune and blood pressure regulation, and inflammation control; it plays a role in our sleep-wake cycle. We need cortisol.

On the negative side, anxiety, stress, and worry release cortisol. Anxiety, stress, and worry are different from fight-or-flight situations. Humans tend to self-inflict anxiety, worry, and stress, and we do this at high levels. When cortisol is released in doses that exceed what is beneficial, it can lead to impaired memory, weakened immunity, depression, and weight gain. Recent studies associate excessive levels of cortisol with an increased risk of certain cancers, such as breast, prostate, and colon cancer.

Adrenaline can also affect our bodies in both positive and negative ways. Like cortisol, on the positive side, it helps the body respond to stress or danger, preparing it for fight-or-flight situations, heightened awareness, decreased pain sensitivity, and improved memory.

On the negative side, anxiety, stress, and worry release adrenaline. Anxiety, stress, and worry are different from fight-or-flight situations. Humans tend to self-inflict anxiety, worry, and stress, and we do this at high levels. When adrenaline is released in doses that exceed what is beneficial, it can lead to high blood pressure, heart palpitations, increased risk of heart attack, headaches, difficulty concentrating, and impaired memory. Next, let's look at serotonin, dopamine, and oxytocin.

Anxiety, stress, and worry significantly disrupt the production and regulation of the three essential chemicals; serotonin, dopamine, and oxytocin.

Serotonin is a neurotransmitter that helps regulate mood, sleep, appetite, digestion, and learning, and low levels are linked to depression. We do not want to disrupt the natural release of this chemical.

Dopamine, often known as the "feel-good" hormone, is a neurotransmitter that is part of the brain's reward system associated with pleasure, motivation, and learning. We have to be very careful with dopamine. We can trick our bodies into releasing it by seeking and acting on behaviors that release it. Dopamine is associated with addictions like gambling, sex, drinking, drug use, food consumption, and even the little beeps and dings of our cell phones. We can get addicted to the release of dopamine by indulging in these activities. Its intended purpose is motivation and procreation.

Oxytocin, often called the "love hormone," is crucial in social bonding, reducing stress and depression, and building trust. It is released during physical touch, social interaction, activities like labor, breastfeeding, and sexual activity, as well as during moments of relaxation and bonding. Unlike dopamine, we cannot get addicted to oxytocin.

Acting morally releases helpful chemicals. Acting immorally releases harmful chemicals. Acting immorally interferes with the release of essential, helpful chemicals. These five chemicals help us determine when a person is acting in leadership. Let's learn how.

Eating healthily is right and just. Eating unhealthily is a sin. We have not been taught to view concepts like our health and relationships through this lens. We talk in terms of doing evil to others without realizing that we sin and do evil to ourselves by intentionally damaging our bodies slowly over time.

Eating crappy foods releases dopamine. However, the feeling we get at the moment is temporary. We eat to feel good, then we feel crappy soon after. We have the ability to understand this and act in a manner that doesn't allow our bodies to trick us into doing unhealthy things.

Would you agree that people who eat healthily and exercise are acting in leadership? I have yet to meet a person who says "no" to that question. Do you think a person who eats unhealthily and does not exercise, which leads to poor health, has acted in leadership? I have yet to meet a person who says "yes" to that question.

We need context about what sin and evil mean. Proverbs talks about not hanging out with people who sin or do evil. Does that mean not associating with just murderers and thieves? No. We have science today that tells us that when we hang around with people with bad habits, we are almost guaranteed to exhibit those same habits.

Hang out with gamblers, and you're likely to gamble. Gambling tricks our bodies into releasing dopamine. Dopamine's primary purpose is motivation. Set a goal, complete a task, and you get some dopamine. It's about being productive and contributing to society. When we abuse this universal chemical, we are sinning. We are going against the foundational principles and scientific universal laws illustrated through these chemicals. "Do not gamble" is good advice.

Throughout the Book of Proverbs, we gain insight on what happens when we disregard good advice, the lessons of wisdom, and the benefits of wisdom.

We come full circle back to Proverbs 3:1-2 and how wisdom bestows well-being. We cannot force someone to eat healthily, exercise, save money, stop gambling, or stop spending foolishly. Becoming obese and going into debt both create stress in our lives, interfering with the release of essential beneficial chemicals and releasing excessive levels of damaging chemicals. Stop doing that and live a longer, more peaceful life.

*Wisdom Bestows Well-Being*

> *My son, do not forget my teaching,*
> *but keep my commands in your heart,*
> *for they will prolong your life many years*
> *and bring you peace and prosperity*
> ~Proverbs 3:1-2 (NIV)

Do you agree that a person who saves a little money and spends wisely is acting in leadership? I have yet to meet a person who says "no" to that question. The *Bible* contains countless life lessons, including teachings on health and finances. We can now see why defining when a person is acting in leadership is the most effective way to determine when a person is a leader.

Also, these verses contain language about God, faithfulness, and trust in the Lord. In my opinion, people get distracted by that language and miss the lessons or are driven away from the *Bible* because of their mindset about the *Bible* and religion in general.

We'll address this language in upcoming chapters. We're working our way through what appears to be a high level of complexity when most of the *Bible* is not complex at all. What might appear as more obscure language will not make sense if we do not understand the basics first.

Proverbs 17:22 addresses how having a positive attitude is healthy.

> *A cheerful heart is good medicine,*
> *but a crushed spirit dries up the bones.*
> ~Proverbs 17:22 (NIV)

A cheerful heart describes a person's state of mind. A crushed spirit addresses a person's belief about the possibility of having hope. A person believing that it's too late to change the way they live is a crushed spirit. Today, we talk in terms of our beliefs and our mindset.

Proverbs 23:17-21, shown below, teaches us a lesson about who we envy. Envy is wishing you had what another person has. You are resentful of an advantage enjoyed by another, combined with a desire to possess the same advantage.

*Saying 15*

*Do not let your heart envy sinners,*

*but always be zealous for the fear of the LORD.*
*There is surely a future hope for you,*
  *and your hope will not be cut off.*

## Saying 16

*Listen, my son, and be wise,*
  *and set your heart on the right path:*
*Do not join those who drink too much wine*
  *or gorge themselves on meat,*
*for drunkards and gluttons become poor,*
  *and drowsiness clothes them in rags.*
~Proverbs 23:17-21 (NIV)

This passage talks about not envying sinners. Why only sinners? We should not envy anyone. Envy falls on the negative side of the leadership lifeline. Envy of what others possess detracts from our ability to be grateful for what we already have. When people practice being grateful for what they already have, this removes stress from their lives by removing the emotion of envy.

Remember, envy means you are resentful of an advantage enjoyed by another, combined with a desire to possess the same advantage. All of that causes anxiety, stress, and a state of discontentment. So again, why does this passage in the *Bible* specifically say "sinners?"

It's the same as any modern-day book that provides a lesson to illustrate a point. When we look at all the books of the *Bible*, the concept of envy is addressed many times in various books. Each of those instances discusses envy in a unique way. We would find the same thing in today's world. Pick up one book, and they illustrate a specific lesson about envy. The next book might talk about a different attribute of envy, but it is always about how envy is a negative thing. Here's a modern-day story that combines envy and sinning.

Gangsters and gangs try to portray their lives as being really cool. We know gangsters sin. It's pretty much the mantra of their lifestyle. Kill, steal, lie, deceive, and sell drugs, just to name a few. Yet, some envy their lifestyle, perhaps a kid whose life appears to have little meaning. Their family struggles day to day to make ends meet. Things can look very hopeless.

These youngsters might view the life of a gang member as better than theirs. They resent the fact that the gang members are rewarded for doing bad things. Remember, envy means you are resentful of an advantage enjoyed by another, combined with a desire to possess the same advantage. In the case of gangs and gang members, in order to have what they have, you end up doing the same bad things that they did.

Do not envy sinners. It will take you down an undesirable path in life. You can get sucked into that world of violence and illegal activities. It's a simple lesson. Some *Bible* passages address not envying people for their wealth and status. That is also bad.

Again, when we talk about sins or sinning, we think in terms of committing murder, stealing, etc. We miss how it pertains to what we tend to see as small, insignificant things. A sin or sinning is anything that will not pass through the integrity hub and lands on the negative side of the leadership lifeline. Defining it that way allows us to achieve clarity when we look at passages in the *Bible*.

# CHAPTER EIGHT

# BASIC™ Leadership In The *Bible*

I consider myself very fortunate to have gained the insight to create the Loop of Optimal Effectiveness and the BASIC Leadership blueprint. I was blessed, but it wasn't luck. Both of those inventions and this book, *The Bible Teaches Acting In Leadership*, came into existence because of how the components of the BASIC Leadership blueprint work.

I believed in a worthy ideal. I acted upon it. I progressed, sometimes forward and sometimes backward, meaning I succeeded or didn't succeed at a certain point during the progression. I gained insight and put the insight to use. I collaborated with others. I constantly moved from one component to another. When my beliefs, actions, progressions, insight, and collaborations passed the integrity test and existed on the positive side of the leadership lifeline, I was acting in leadership, thereby a leader at that time.

Lucius Annaeus Seneca was a Roman philosopher born over two thousand years ago in 1 BCE. Seneca said;

> *Luck is what happens when*
> *preparation meets opportunity.*

People who act in leadership are not lucky. It's the BASIC components at work. When a person enacts the five elements of the outer ring in the BASIC Leadership blueprint, they will be prepared when an opportunity presents itself.

Every single one of the BASIC leadership blueprint components is illustrated in the *Bible*.

Let's begin with belief. The word believe is mentioned around 250 times in the *Bible*, but this concept is actually addressed at a much higher level than that. We tend to mentally tie the word "faith" to the idea of being religious. Let's compare the definition of belief to the definition of faith.

- ➢ Belief: trust, faith, or confidence in someone or something.
- ➢ Faith: complete trust or confidence in someone or something.

There is no difference between saying, "I believe _____." and "I have faith in _____."

The word "belief" has many synonyms, words that mean exactly or nearly the same thing. Beliefs are being addressed when we see words such as faith, think, and mindset.

The word "faith" appears over 200 times in the *Bible*, depending on which translation is used. That means that the concept of beliefs appears at least 450 times in the *Bible*.

> *He replied, "Because you have so little faith. Truly I tell you, if you have faith as small as a mustard seed, you can say to this mountain, 'Move from here to there,' and it will move. Nothing will be impossible for you."*
> ~Matthew 17:20 (NIV)

Moving mountains is an analogy. We can do incredible things when we believe something is possible. Earlier, we learned about the parable of the mustard seed. We learned that little things matter as much as big things. Little things turn into big things, whether good or bad. Do you believe that? Not believing it is also a belief. I believe it. I have faith that it is true. Therefore, I act based on that belief. Whatever I believe, I become more of that. We'll address the concept of becoming more of what you believe in chapter fifteen, Meditation, Affirmations, and Prayer.

Whatever you believe will drive the actions you take or do not take. To act means to do something, to make progress. We constantly take action. Doing nothing is also taking an action. It's the action of doing nothing.

> *Blessed are those who act justly,*
> *who always do what is right.*
> ~Psalm 106:3 (NIV)

The Book of Psalms, chapter 106, verse 3, gives us a specific type of action—an action that passes the integrity test and exists on the positive side of the leadership lifeline: to "act justly" and "do what is right." Are you starting to see how these things all fit together and how they form the BASIC Leadership blueprint?

In chapter sixteen, we'll dig into the concept of worry. Did worrying ever pay the bills? Did worrying ever fix anything in your life? No. That's because worrying is not an action, it is an emotion. Let's keep going.

> *Ask and it will be given to you; seek and you will*
> *find; knock and the door will be opened to you. For*
> *everyone who asks receives; the one who seeks*
> *finds; and to the one who knocks, the door will be*
> *opened.*
> ~Matthew 7:7-8 (NIV)

Everything in this passage, Matthew 7:7-8, requires an action. Those actions will be based on a belief.

Next, let's look at the component of success.

Every action drives a progression, good or bad. Progression exists within the "success" component of the BASIC Leadership blueprint. Why I chose the word success and how it is defined becomes extremely important.

We can find passages that contain the words success and progress.

> *Keep this Book of the Law always on your lips; meditate on it day and night, so that you may be careful to do everything written in it. Then you will be prosperous and successful.*
> ~Joshua 1:8 (NIV)

> *Be diligent in these matters; give yourself wholly to them, so that everyone may see your progress.*
> ~1 Timothy 4:15 (NIV)

Again, we can find passages containing those words, but like the action component, the word action does not have to exist for us to see that a verse is about taking action.

Similarly, the words success or progress do not have to exist in any passage for us to understand that those actions are a progression in some direction, good or bad.

The first Book of Timothy, chapter 4, verse 15, shown above, tells us to live the lesson first. To demonstrate "by doing," not just by talking about it. The concept of a progression is illustrated within the verses using other words like path and direction. The analogy of walking down a path means we are headed somewhere, toward something. Getting there is a progression. The word "path" appears hundreds of times in the *Bible*. We see it here in the Book of Proverbs, chapter 4, verse 26.

> *Give careful thought to the paths for your feet*
> *and be steadfast in all your ways.*
> ~Proverbs 4:26 (NIV)

Again, anytime we provide context, it all makes sense. Chapter 4 in the Book of Proverbs is titled "Get Wisdom at Any Cost." The wisdom illustrated here is "to be righteous," to live with integrity and on the positive side of the leadership lifeline. We see this in verses 18 and 19 leading up to verse 26.

> *The path of the righteous is like the morning sun,*
> *shining ever brighter till the full light of day.*
> *But the way of the wicked is like deep darkness;*
> *they do not know what makes them stumble.*
> ~Proverbs 4:18-19 (NIV)

Notice that the word path appears here as well. What path? What direction are we taking in life? How will we progress in life? In a good way or bad way? Not in terms of did we hit some arbitrary goal but in terms of how we live, behave, and act.

That covers the component of success. Let's look at insight.

Wisdom is having good sense and sound judgment. It requires insight: The capacity to gain an accurate and intuitive understanding. The word insight appears in the *Bible* at least 39 times, and wisdom appears over 200 times.

> *Counsel and sound judgment are mine;*
> *I have insight, I have power.*
> ~Proverbs 8:14 (NIV)

If the word wisdom appears five times more than insight, why did I choose insight and not wisdom for the BASIC Leadership blueprint? Selecting a component solely on the number of times it appears is not the most effective method. I can manufacture a large quantity of an item, but if it doesn't work when we put the machine together, then the fact that a bunch of them exist becomes irrelevant. I did not select the BASIC Leadership blueprint components solely on how often they appear anywhere.

Each instance of gaining insight leads to wisdom. Wisdom is a broader concept referring to a well-developed understanding of life and the world. We acquire that well-developed understanding of life and the world a little bit at a time. We are not suddenly wise. Becoming wise is a progression. Gain some insight here and gain some insight there, and we become wiser.

Every time a *Bible* verse tells us to "understand," that's the equivalent of gaining insight. When we compare any two versions of the *Bible*, for instance, the

New King James Version (NKJV) and the New International Version (NIV), we see one uses the word "understanding" and the other uses "insight." The word "understand" is mentioned around 89 times in the *Bible*.

> *Counsel and sound judgment are mine;*
> *I have insight, I have power.*
> ~Proverbs 8:14 (NIV)

> *Counsel is mine, and sound wisdom;*
> *I am understanding, I have strength.*
> ~Proverbs 8:14 (NKJV)

For the last eight years, I have been trying to poke holes in the BASIC leadership blueprint, to find weaknesses and flaws, to see if there was a more effective way to define acting in leadership. It's held up to everything I've thrown at it. Is it perfect? Oh, heck no. But every time I illustrate how it works, all the components fit together like a well-made puzzle. It provides a straightforward way to explain how life generally works and what it means to act in leadership. It has been the most effective way to enact the third stage of the loop of optimal effectiveness when it comes to defining when a person is a leader.

I do not want you to take what I present as the only way life and leadership work. But one has to admit, it's pretty freaking good. And all seven components exist in the *Bible*. Let's look at collaboration.

When we gain insight, take action, and progress toward something, collaborating with someone or something almost always takes place. To collaborate means to join with someone or something to create. When we think of creating something, we tend to think of physical objects. We create thoughts and beliefs, neither of which can be seen or felt.

How does collaboration happen when you acquire a new belief? You collaborated with someone or something for that to happen. A new insight can be gained by observing nature. You collaborated with nature.

Other ways to describe collaboration are cooperating, working together, participating, combining, and uniting. The word "collaborate" first appeared in the English language around the 1870s, originating from the Latin verb "collabōrāre," which means "to work together." The following passage addresses collaboration.

*Imitate Christ's Humility*

*Therefore, if you have any encouragement from being united with Christ, if any comfort from his love, if any common sharing in the Spirit, if any tenderness and compassion, then make my joy complete by being like-minded, having the same love, being one in spirit and of one mind. Do nothing out of selfish ambition or vain conceit. Rather, in humility value others above yourselves, not looking to your own interests but*

*each of you to the interests of the others.*
~ Philippians 2:1-4 (NIV)

I chose this verse because it is more complex than many other verses about collaboration. It tells us a lot more than that, and an incredible story is behind it.

First, the language of "common sharing" is collaboration. The wording "like-minded" does not mean everyone should act like robots and not think for themselves. Like-mindedness refers to how everyone should live with integrity and on the positive side of the leadership lifeline. We should agree on that approach to life. Is there anyone who argues against us all living our lives this way? Sadly, the answer is yes. But leadership coaches do not teach us that.

The apostle Paul wrote letters to the Philippians while he was in prison. Paul was in jail for preaching the gospel of Christ. Wait a second! When we look at the lessons Jesus taught, lessons such as "be humble." Did you know that people went to prison for teaching these things? They did.

Paul was teaching lessons that the Pharisees found threatening to their authority. The Pharisees were the people who were supposed to be leading the churches. They were supposed to help those in need and help people live rightly. Instead, they thought that following 612 rules and regulations, mostly man-made misinterpretations of the *Bible*, was their purpose. Rather than helping people, they judged people who did not adhere to all these rules.

Then, Jesus shows up and begins to teach the real lessons of life and what it means to act in leadership. Jesus' actions and lessons threaten their authority; Jesus is not a Pharisee, and according to them, he doesn't have authority.

Paul was sharing the teachings of Jesus, so they arrested him. Yet, while in prison, Paul still worked to pass on these principles, the lessons of acting in leadership.

Paul tells the Philippians they must collaborate and work together to "Do nothing out of selfish ambition or vain conceit. Rather, in humility value others above yourselves, not looking to your own interests but each of you to the interests of the others." The Pharisees looked out only for their own self-ambitions.

Practicing humility is a worthy ideal and will be a continuous progression. The title of this chapter in the Book of Philippians is "Imitating Christ's Humility." Many modern-day TED Talks contain lessons about the importance of humility and how it is a leadership trait. There's an entire chapter about it in just one of the books of the *Bible*.

Yes, one of the reasons for Paul's imprisonment is that he was claiming Jesus to be the Messiah. This was a big problem for the Pharisees, but the lessons that Jesus passed on also threatened their ritualistic practices and their power. Paul was imprisoned for both.

If the people who give these TED Talks today did that in 61 AD, they could have been imprisoned if they did not stop teaching these same principles. Paul would not stop, so he was put in jail. Imagine Roman guards rushing the stage at a modern-day TED Talk and arresting someone. There's a scary image for you to ponder.

If that happened to you, would you start writing letters about this humility principle and send them to people in nearby cities? That is commitment!

When discussions about the *Bible* arise, I've heard people say, "It's just a book." I used to nod in agreement. What do you think or believe now? That brings us to the components of Integrity and the Leadership Lifeline.

Acting with integrity and living on the positive side of the leadership lifeline are referenced in abundance in all 66 books of the *Bible*. The *Bible* constantly addresses positive and negative, good and evil, moral and immoral.

> *Better is a poor person who walks in his integrity*
> *than one who is perverse in his lips, and is a fool.*
> ~Proverbs 19:1 (NKJV)

The Book of Proverbs, chapter 19, tells us it's better to be poor and live with integrity than to be a scumbag and be wealthy. I could fill a hundred pages with examples addressing integrity and positive versus negative.

Let's see a passage that ties multiple components of the BASIC Leadership blueprint together.

> *His divine power has given us everything we need*
> *for a godly life through our knowledge of him who*
> *called us by his own glory and goodness. Through*

*these he has given us his very great and precious
promises, so that through them you may participate
in the divine nature, having escaped the corruption
in the world caused by evil desires.*

*For this very reason, make every effort to add to
your faith goodness; and to goodness,
knowledge; and to knowledge, self-control; and to
self-control, perseverance; and to perseverance,
godliness; and to godliness, mutual affection; and to
mutual affection, love. For if you possess these
qualities in increasing measure, they will keep you
from being ineffective and unproductive in your
knowledge of our Lord Jesus Christ. But whoever
does not have them is nearsighted and
blind, forgetting that they have been cleansed from
their past sins.*
~ 2 Peter 1:3–9 (NIV)

In the second paragraph, we see "make every effort." That's taking action. "Adding knowledge" is gaining insight. "In increasing measure" is a progression. "Add to your faith goodness" means believing that acting with integrity and on the positive side of the leadership lifeline is the right thing to do. It talks about being "effective" in how we live our lives, bringing the loop of optimal effectiveness into the equation.

The lessons presented in the *Bible* are associated with one or more of the seven BASIC Leadership blueprint components. Now that you are aware of how the *Bible* addresses all seven elements of the BASIC Leadership blueprint, it'll become more apparent as we work through each chapter. Here are the components for review.

**Back to BASIC™**
Leadership Platform

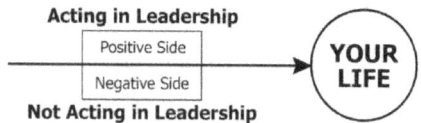

**Back to BASIC™**
Leadership Life Line
© Scott M Carter 2017

# CHAPTER NINE

# Reframing The Picture

Once upon a time... there was a petite yet strong-willed woman of seventeen who embarked on a journey to free her people from oppression that had lasted almost one hundred years.

She would accomplish astonishing things. For instance, she said that God told her about the existence and location of an ancient sword hidden under the altar of St. Catherine's at Fierbois. High priests well-versed in history and artifacts had no knowledge or awareness of the weapon's existence. Yet, the sword was there, as she predicted.

This seventeen-year-old girl could not read or write. Despite being illiterate, she outwitted scholars with years of schooling, practice in debate, and expertise in the art of philosophy. Despite her many accomplishments, she was never prideful and did not seek power or recognition.

Many who wanted to attain or retain power would oppose her, including those within her own country who held distinguished titles. Despite this fierce opposition, she won the hearts of the people and gave them new hope.

She became the commander of an army, answering only to the king. She rode on a white horse dressed in shiny silver armor, carrying the small sacred sword of Fierbois, always at the forefront of any assault of those who sought to oppress others. Yet, throughout all these battles, she never killed one person.

That introduction could be the beginning of one of the *Star Wars* movies, a large yellow font scrolling up the screen, setting the stage for what we are about to see.

Imagine yourself as her rival on the other side of these fierce encounters. Your army consists of rugged, manly men capable of wielding the most enormous swords and weapons. At the head of the pack charging toward you is a petite young teenage woman with a sword half the size of the ones your men are wielding.

This story of a seventeen-year-old girl sounds like many of the plots of the sci-fi books and movies we love to read and watch. I could mirror this story with a dozen of my favorite sci-fi movies. For instance, it is as if a person were watching one of the Harry Potter series of movies where the sword of Gryffindor would appear to only those with a pure heart and truly in need. Or it is like the scene from the movie *The Hobbit, An Unexpected Journey*, where Bilbo Baggins finds a tiny yet mighty Elven sword that serves him well.

But what could this story and these comparisons possibly have to do with how the *Bible* teaches acting in leadership?

Do you believe these events and the story of this seventeen-year-old are real? Is she real? The answer is yes. Her name is Joan of Arc. She was a real person, unlike all the sci-fi characters who do amazing things. It was 1429, when Joan was seventeen, and her journey began. Movies have been made about her, and books have been written about her. One book in particular provides us with the most accurate story of her journey.

Mark Twain spent twelve years researching Joan of Arc's life and background to create a magnificent literary work aptly named *Joan of Arc*, which was published in 1896. Most people know Twain for *Huckleberry Finn* and *Tom Sawyer*, both novels about fictional characters.

Like other fans of Twain, I had no idea he had written this book. Twain himself says it was the best book he had ever written. Twain relied on two things.

First, part of Joan of Arc's life story comes to us under oath in a court trial. Joan of Arc was burned at the stake by high-ranking priests and religious officials because she was found guilty in a religious court. Those court records still exist to this day.

Second, her childhood friend, the Sieur Louis de Conte, came from a family of nobility. He could read and write. The Sieur Louis de Conte, her childhood friend, became her page and secretary during this tumultuous part of her life, scribing the events. The Sieur Louis de Conte would survive the battles to live past the age of

82, allowing him to compile his notes and personal recollections of this journey from her childhood innocence to the fire that consumed her life. The events listed above are accurate, including the fact that she knew the location of the sacred sword of Fierbois when no other person did. How can a person explain that?

People recorded events from Joan's life, and the 66 books of the *Bible* also exist because people recorded those events and shared stories. In the previous chapters, we learned the importance of context and how to deal with complexity. We may not have realized it, but we were reframing how we see things.

We reframe in many areas of our lives when things seem confusing. Psychologists refer to this technique as cognitive reframing. In fact, reframing the way we look at things is a strategy taught in many leadership courses. You've seen it presented as "changing our perspective" or "a paradigm shift," as Stephen Covey calls it. Covey wrote the book *The 7 Habits of Highly Effective People*.

People often struggle with the language in the *Bible*. In this and the next chapter, we will reframe some wording and address some misconceptions because they are taken out of context. Here is a list of challenges we have discussed and will continue to address.

- ✓ The stories aren't real. People just made things up.
- ✓ People don't think it's relative to their life. "I'm not religious. It's only for religious people."

✓ People think they must attend church or join a religious organization to understand the *Bible*.

✓ People fear what others might think if they say that they read and follow the lessons of the *Bible*. "Oh, you're one of those people."

✓ People who attend church, claim to be religious, and talk about what's in the *Bible, yet* do not seem to live by the standards they preach. The appearance of being hypocrites.

✓ Some religious people act as if they are superior to others.

✓ If the lessons of the *Bible* are supposed to fix things, why do so many religious people still have the same problems as the rest of us?

✓ The *Bible* isn't easy to understand (level of complexity). I don't know where to start. I don't understand the context of the stories. The language is too hard to relate to.

✓ People think the lessons do not apply in today's world. These are stories and unrealistic representations of life from the Stone Age. What could a bunch of donkey-riding barbarians have to teach us?

When you read the preceding story about Joan of Arc, specifically the part where she tells everyone how she knew about the sacred sword of Fierbois and how God told her where it was, what was your reaction to that statement?

Let's see another example since you may not remember how you reacted to that statement. Read the following question.

*What keeps you from reading God's word?*

What immediate emotion or response does this language elicit? If you go to church and believe in God, the response can be more simplistic with answers like, "I don't have time." But, if you are a person who is not of any religious faith, then some or all of the things in the above list could be the reason.

Let's address the words "God," "Lord," and "Christ." A person might think that the language is too hard to understand, and that going to church, being religious, and believing in a higher power are required.

Wording like "God" and "the Lord" creates a mindset that it is only for people who are religious and only about religion. If a person does not believe in any higher power, these stories and lessons cannot be real. God is just some invisible man in the sky.

Because of this mindset, which is simply due to the lack of a way to view some of the *Bible*'s language, many people are missing out on the lessons of acting in leadership. Let's examine how others have overcome some of these challenges.

If you are not familiar with Glenn Beck, his radio program is one of the top-rated radio shows in the country. In other words, lots of people listen to his broadcasts. He's very spiritual and interviews a lot of intellectual, science-driven people. Think of him as a radio version of the Joe Rogan podcasts.

The following is from a Glenn Beck interview with Astrophysicist Hugh Ross. Ross presented his viewpoint and arrived at a different way to look at labels such as God and Lord in the *Bible*. I will bullet-point it to make it easy to follow.

- Hugh Ross is an astrophysicist who studies the universe.
- His research tells him that the beginning of the universe favors a big bang.
- Therefore, Ross agrees that the universe has a beginning.
- If the universe has a beginning, there must be a cosmic beginner. Ross, through the *Bible*, understood the cosmic beginner to be God.
- Ross was invited to a government lab to present his research on scientific astrophysics. The problem is that the facilitators told him that the US Government does not allow the use of the word "God" in any scientific presentation.
- Ross had to come up with an alternative. He used cognitive reframing and relabeled the word God as "the causal agent beyond space and time." Reframing the language solved the problem.

He's not the only one who found another method for addressing specific language within the *Bible*. Glenn Beck and Hugh Ross have something in common. When Glenn Beck wanted to learn about God and the *Bible*, his dad told him that the first thing he needed to do was get rid of the word "God." The reason? The word means too many things and has too many traps to fall into. His dad gave him the insight to refer to God as "First Cause."

So, we have a discussion between an astrophysicist and a highly spiritual person. These are both very intelligent people. Both of their approaches to dealing with the language in the *Bible* are to find another way to define it so they do not lose sight of their main objective. They use cognitive reframing to address the language. Ross' objective was to explain that someone or something had to light the match to ignite the Big Bang. Beck's objective was to learn about the lessons of the *Bible*.

My objective in this book is to illustrate how the *Bible* teaches acting in leadership. I want to focus on that and not go down rabbit hole debates about an all-powerful God versus the Big Bang versus evolution.

People tend to think in terms of "either/or" when we debate things. Our world is from the Big Bang, or an existential higher power created it. Why can't it be both? What lit the match if the Big Bang is correct, and everything came from nothing? What set off the Big Bang? That was the question that Astrophysicist Hugh Ross asked himself. He had to come up with another name. We can even take it a step further and combine all three, saying "something lit the match, there was a big bang, and things evolved from there." Instead, we argue which one is correct: a First Cause, aka a singular creator, a big bang, or evolution.

If you argue against reframing the word God with the label First Cause, you're arguing against using the word God. YHWH is the correct name or label. It's pronounced "Yah-Way." That has been replaced with the word or label God. It's already been reframed.

Again, the argument about the Big Bang or not, the argument for or against a higher power, is not what we're discussing here. We're learning about how the *Bible* teaches acting in leadership, and some of the language can create confusion and distractions, taking us down other paths away from the objective – how the *Bible* teaches acting in leadership.

We are not changing the *Bible* when we view some of the language through a different filter. The facts, stories, and lessons are the same. We are reframing some of the words and language. This approach is very common. We do this in other areas of our lives when things seem confusing.

Glenn Beck and Astrophysicist Hugh Ross are using cognitive reframing. Let's continue.

In the *Bible...*

- God refers to the creator (First Cause).
- Jesus is a real person.
- Christ is another name for Jesus.
- Lord is another name for both God and Jesus.

When we see the words, God or Lord, we can mentally replace them with The First Cause. I like The First Cause because the universe has consistent scientific laws that apply to everything. Here are some examples.

Newton's law of motion and his law of gravitation. The laws of thermodynamics. And Ohm's law. Ohm's law states that the current flowing through a conductor between two points is directly proportional to the potential difference between the two points and inversely proportional to the resistance between the two points.

Because we understand Ohm's law, we can correctly install electrical power in our homes and businesses. Universal laws help us understand how universal intelligence is organized. Because there is so much science regarding universal laws, experts are now agreeing that there is a singular intelligence behind the overall design of the universe.

We have proof that there are intelligent universal designs. In chapters three and seven, we became aware of the chemicals cortisol, adrenaline, oxytocin, serotonin, and dopamine. These are punishment and reward chemicals assigned to different types of human behavior. They are released based on universal laws associated with positive and negative behaviors, just like the laws that govern the positive and negative sides of electricity.

In chapter eight, we reframed the word "faith" because it means the same thing as belief.

➢ Belief: Trust, faith, or confidence in someone or something.
➢ Faith: Complete trust or confidence in someone or something.

Scientists have faith. Faith in what? Faith that there are explanations for the way things work. Faith that we can find a cure for things like cancer. Everyone has faith. This human attribute means everyone is a believer in something. It becomes a matter of faith in what or belief in what?

We believe in scientific universal laws, such as the law of gravity, and we also believe in scientific universal laws for behaviors. These foundational principles and scientific universal laws include "do not murder, steal, or lie."

If you're as much of a research nerd as I am, there is a peer-reviewed study by M.B. Dastagiri. The paper focuses on analyzing different universal laws and their origin, rationale, and prophecy. It's titled "Universal Laws, Nature Laws, God Laws, Spiritual, Philosophical & Science Laws: Origin, Rationales, Prophesy, and Human Well-Being." Look it up and read through it.

In chapter three, I mentioned my book, *Back To BASIC™: Acting In Leadership*. We learned that four different cultures used nature metaphors and analogies to understand and illustrate the principles of life: the *Dhammapada*, the teachings of Buddha from India, the *Tao Te Ching*, the teachings of Lao Tzu from China, philosophers like Aristotle, Plato, and Socrates, and, of course, the *Bible*. All four cultures believed that natural universal principles and laws existed, illustrating how to live our lives.

This multicultural understanding cannot simply be a coincidence. Multiple cultures that existed thousands of years ago, thousands of miles apart, all came to the same conclusion: there are universal principles and laws that show us the right way to live.

Today, we have a ton of science regarding universal principles and laws. Remember, we're not rewriting the *Bible*. The lessons will not change when we take this approach. We are also not proving nor dismissing the existence of a higher power. I am simply pointing out what others are finding through scientific research: these are universal principles and laws, and they have to come from somewhere. These universal principles and laws are by design.

We're reframing the language of God with a primary intelligent source, a First Cause. Give it whatever label you like. Don't let it detract from how the *Bible* teaches acting in leadership.

When we encounter the word Jesus, we don't have to change anything. Jesus was a real person, just like Joan of Arc. He presented life lessons, the lessons of acting in leadership.

If I say to be more like Jesus or, as Dr. Wayne Dyer says, Christ-like, we are to follow the lessons Jesus taught. And if we follow the premise that Jesus was the son of God, a son of First Cause, then that gives us another way to look at his teaching. Jesus got instructions for the proper way to live from whoever lit the match—First Cause. Jesus is teaching us the universal laws of acting in leadership.

Now, we can revisit the *Bible* passage we used in chapter seven to examine the language of divine power, knowledge of God, and obedience to Christ.

> *For though we live in the world, we do not wage war as the world does. The weapons we fight with are not the weapons of the world. On the contrary, they have divine power to demolish strongholds. We demolish arguments and every pretension that sets itself up against the knowledge of God, and we take captive every thought to make it obedient to Christ.*
> ~2 Corinthians 10:3-5 (NIV)

What universal law and lesson is 2 Corinthians 10:3-5 addressing? The law of attraction.

The Law of Attraction states that positive thoughts bring positive results into a person's life, while negative thoughts bring negative outcomes. We have hundreds of studies to back up this universal law. Let's break this passage down into bullet points.

- The universal law is "The Law of Attraction."
- We can demolish all the evil thoughts that have a stronghold on us.
- Negative thoughts cannot hold up against the remedy of using positive thoughts.

- Our power to enact this principle comes from one primary source: the First Cause (divine power) (knowledge of God).
- It's a universal law that anyone can apply to their life.
- Jesus taught this universal law thousands of years ago; we should follow his advice (obedient to Christ).

When you remove certain biblical labels, this bullet point list looks just like any lesson a modern-day leadership coach puts on a screen during a TED Talk. If you went to a presentation that teaches this lesson, it likely developed out of the lessons of the *Bible*.

I could write a book with hundreds of passages from the *Bible* and then connect those passages to modern-day leadership lessons, which are also universal principles and laws that apply to all of us. But how effective would that be if we did not address why people might avoid the *Bible* and its teachings?

Now, when you encounter *Bible* passages and verses with language that might be difficult to comprehend or relate to, you can reframe them into a modern-day leadership presentation format.

# CHAPTER TEN

# *Bible* Misconceptions

There are many misconceptions about the *Bible*. In the early chapters of this book, we addressed what I would consider the biggest misconception of them all: that the *Bible* is just some large book full of weird stories, all made up, way too hard to comprehend, something missionaries took on long trips to exotic countries or a large moral superiority weapon people used to whack others over the head.

We also addressed a few other misconceptions.

- The *Bible* is always literal. No, it uses parables, analogies, and metaphors.
- There is only one way to interpret it or the lessons presented. No, passages can teach multiple lessons.
- To understand or apply any of it, you need to be religious and understand all of it. No, a

person does not have to be religious. The *Bible* teaches acting in leadership. You can apply any lesson once you understand that lesson.

Humans have been adding clarification to things for centuries and still do it today. A misconception is an incorrect point of view because we don't understand the context in which it was presented.

I have attended dozens of corporate trainings and leadership presentations. During those presentations, it is common for the speaker to say, "Let me clarify," followed by an explanation. The speaker wants to ensure that you have the right context and do not misinterpret the lesson or point being made.

We'll go deeper into each one of the following misconceptions.

1. The *Bible* is 100% fact.
2. The *Bible* is a rule book.
3. The *Bible* has an answer for everything.
4. The *Bible* is full of contradictions.
5. God is like a genie in a magic lamp that grants wishes.
6. The *Bible* promises that bad things won't happen.
7. If this stuff works, why aren't the people who go to church perfect?
8. Church and religion are about rituals that make people puppets, controlling them.
9. Money is the root of all evil.

10. The *Bible* tells us it's okay to take revenge.

## Misconception #1: The Bible is 100% fact.

No. It contains parables, analogies, and metaphors. Many of the stories are accounts of actual events and lives. No different than what takes place today; people write about other people and events. Those stories are from the perspective of the person writing about them.

## Misconception #2: The Bible contradicts itself so that discounts all of it.

Yes, of course, there are potential contradictions. It's 66 books produced over 1,500 years, written in 3 languages, across 3 continents, by 40 unique authors. I have shelves full of leadership books. Different authors often contradict each other, and some contradict themselves in just one book. Why do we try to hold the *Bible* to a different standard?

Ask any law enforcement person who interviews witnesses from a scene. You get the same story from different perspectives. That does not mean an event did not take place. When we look closer, we'll see that no matter which perspective, the lesson remains the same. I'll provide an example of the same story from two perspectives. John and Matthew were both present at the same time and wrote about this event in their own books.

*Jesus entered the temple courts and drove out all who were buying and selling there. He overturned the tables of the money changers and the benches of*

*those selling doves. "It is written," he said to them, "My house will be called a house of prayer, but you are making it a den of robbers."*
~ Matthew 21:12-13 (NIV)

*When it was almost time for the Jewish Passover, Jesus went up to Jerusalem. In the temple courts he found people selling cattle, sheep and doves, and others sitting at tables exchanging money. So he made a whip out of cords, and drove all from the temple courts, both sheep and cattle; he scattered the coins of the money changers and overturned their tables. To those who sold doves he said, "Get these out of here! Stop turning my Father's house into a market!" His disciples remembered that it is written: "Zeal for your house will consume me."*
~John 2:13-17 (NIV)

Because Matthew didn't mention whips made out of cords, as John told us, doesn't mean he didn't also see it or that it didn't happen.

Whether you believe in God or not, the lesson is that churches have a specific purpose, and that purpose does not include turning it into a marketplace, especially bringing animals inside that poop and pee all over the place. They wrote about the event from their perspective, but the lesson did not change. Focus on the lesson.

Just a heads up. Don't run down to your church and start overturning tables and yelling *Bible* verses because they have a fundraiser in the lunch room or gymnasium. That's not what this lesson implies you should do. You're not living in 29 AD in Jerusalem.

When we see what appear to be significant contradictions, it's because we have not gained insight through context. For instance, if slavery is terrible, why did the *Bible* say it's okay? Do you know for sure that the *Bible* says it's okay?

For centuries, from the 1600s through the 1800s, when the United States was being colonized, wealthy landowners paid the travel expenses for others who wanted to go from Europe to America to start a new life. Those people agreed to work for that estate for a period of time to pay off that debt. It's called indentured servitude.

This same practice of paying off a debt existed when the books of the *Bible* were written. The *Bible* addresses multiple subjects using the word slavery. 1) Indentured servitude, 2) chattel slavery, which was and still is the slave trade, and 3) We can be slaves to our desires.

In the Book of Proverbs, Chapter 22, verse 7 addresses both #1 and #3 above.

> *The rich rule over the poor,*
> *and the borrower is slave to the lender.*
> Proverbs 22:7 (NIV)

We can be slaves to our desires, which cause us to become indebted to a lender. What kind of credit card or other debt do you have right now? Most, if not all of that debt is because you desired things, not because you needed them. The word slavery is used to describe all three. You must understand which type is being addressed in any passage you read. We always need context.

## Misconception #3: The Bible is a rule book.

No. It's an instruction manual for how to live life. Philippians 4:3 tells us it's the Book of Life. We'll see more on this in misconception # 5 below.

Murder, lie, steal, or cheat, then nature has built-in mechanisms to tell us this is wrong. We feel guilt and shame. The *Bible* also tells us what causes anxiety, worry, and stress. Most of it is self-induced by fears like FOMO: Fear Of Missing Out. As we learned in chapter seven, nature has provided an array of chemicals that help us to determine when we act rightly or wrongly. They are cortisol, adrenaline, dopamine, serotonin, and oxytocin. Our bodies are punished or rewarded according to our actions.

## Misconception #4: The Bible has an answer for everything.

No. This one is simple. No person, and indeed no single book, has an answer for everything. But the *Bible* sure as heck has the answer for many things. Most, if not all, of the life lessons we see in modern-day leadership books exist in the *Bible*.

## Misconception #5: God is like a Genie in a magic lamp. You can have whatever you ask for.

We must always read the entire chapter; sometimes, we must read two or more chapters together to ensure we understand the lesson through proper context. Grabbing random verses out of the *Bible* and spouting some "out of context" garbage is what leads to misconceptions.

In the Book of John, chapter 14, verses 13 and 14 might appear to suggest that a person can ask for anything and "poof" it will somehow appear or eventually show up.

> *And I will do whatever you ask in my name, so that the Father may be glorified in the Son. You may ask me for anything in my name, and I will do it.*
> ~John 14:13-14 (NIV)

However, when we read the entire chapter, verses 25 to 27 clarify what verses 13 and 14 tell us.

> *All this I have spoken while still with you. But the Advocate, the Holy Spirit, whom the Father will send in my name, will teach you all things and will remind you of everything I have said to you. Peace I leave with you; my peace I give you. I do not give to*

*you as the world gives. Do not let your hearts be*
*troubled and do not be afraid.*
~John 14:25-27 (NIV)

Verse 27 states, "I do not give to you as the world gives." Therefore, not material things or power, etc. When we look at verse 14, it does not say, "You may ask me for anything." It clarifies with "in my name." The universe, the world, does not create the material things or hierarchical power that people seek; people have created those things and concepts.

We make really bad emotional decisions. This is why Proverbs tells us to guard our hearts—to guard our hearts from the desires of the outside world.

*Above all else, guard your heart,*
*for everything you do flows from it.*
~Proverbs 4:23 (NIV)

We see "desires" being addressed repeatedly in the various books of the *Bible.*

*What causes fights and quarrels among you?*
*Don't they come from your desires that*
*battle within you? You desire but do not have, so*
*you kill. You covet but you cannot get what you*
*want, so you quarrel and fight. You do not have*
*because you do not ask God. When you ask, you do*
*not receive, because you ask with wrong*

*motives, that you may spend what you get on your
pleasures.*

~James 4:1-3 (NIV)

We can have peace if we choose to seek it. What kind
of peace? Peace of mind. Peace within our hearts. The
lessons of the *Bible*, of Jesus, constantly illustrate what
causes anxiety, stress, guilt, and shame, then say, "Hey,
don't do these things." Don't violate the integrity hub
and exhibit actions that land on the negative side of the
leadership lifeline. The *Bible* also tells us not to escalate
things, which is different from a natural progression.

The lessons of the *Bible* are about how to live our
lives. How do we know this to be true? Let's look at the
Book of Philippians, chapter 4, verses 1 to 9. It's called
"the Book of Life." Notice the alignment with the
previous passages from John 14:25-27 about being taught
lessons. The Book of Philippians, chapter 4, is very
specific in the last paragraph regarding what the Book of
Life teaches – Whatever is right, pure, and admirable. I
underlined these for you.

*Closing Appeal for Steadfastness and Unity*

*Therefore, my brothers and sisters, you whom I love
and long for, my joy and crown, stand firm in the
Lord in this way, dear friends!*

*I plead with Euodia and I plead with Syntyche to be
of the same mind in the Lord. Yes, and I ask you,*

*my true companion, help these women since they have contended at my side in the cause of the gospel, along with Clement and the rest of my co-workers, whose names are in the <u>book of life.</u>*

*Final Exhortations*

*Rejoice in the Lord always. I will say it again: Rejoice! Let your gentleness be evident to all. The Lord is near. Do not be anxious about anything, but in every situation, by prayer and petition, with thanksgiving, present your requests to God. And the peace of God, which transcends all understanding, will guard your hearts and your minds in Christ Jesus.*

*Finally, brothers and sisters, <u>whatever is true, whatever is noble, whatever is right, whatever is pure, whatever is lovely, whatever is admirable</u>—if anything is excellent or praiseworthy—think about such things. Whatever you have learned or received or heard from me, or seen in me—put it into practice. And the God of peace will be with you.*
~Philippians 4:1-9 (NIV)

We guard our hearts against the desires of this world. We meditate and use affirmations. We pray. We give thanks, meaning we are grateful right now. Then, we must put these things into practice. It says, "put it into practice."

Again, this does not imply we do nothing or live in poverty. Jesus never told the disciples, "Now, go be poor and live in squalor." He did say to detach themselves from material things. Jesus provided lessons on what being "poor" truly means. Lessons on being grateful for what you already have. Lessons about not seeking happiness, joy, or peace in material things. A person can have material wealth and still feel unfulfilled in life. That person is poor in peace of mind, peace of heart. We continue to think of "poor" in terms of money.

## Misconception #6: The Bible promises that bad things won't happen.

The *Bible* is a guide for dealing with the things *that happen*. We say, "Life happens. Deal with it." Ecclesiastes 1 tells us that everything we are experiencing has happened before and will happen again. We think life is more challenging now; we have more problems than people who lived in the past, and so on and so on. We believe that, somehow, by following the lessons within the *Bible*, the challenges we face in life will all go away. The *Bible* does not say this.

> *What has been will be again,*
> *what has been done will be done again;*
> *there is nothing new under the sun.*
> *Is there anything of which one can say,*
> *"Look! This is something new"?*
> *It was here already, long ago;*
> *it was here before our time.*
> *No one remembers the former generations,*
> *and even those yet to come*
> *will not be remembered*

*by those who follow them.*
~ Ecclesiastes 1:9-11 (NIV)

People think some new, magical modern-day innovation will allow us to live a struggle-free life. That will never happen, so you better learn the lessons for dealing with adverse and challenging situations.

## Misconception #7: If this stuff works, why aren't the people who attend church perfect?

No one who goes to church is perfect—in fact, no one on the planet is perfect. Churches are not country clubs for saints. So many of the *Bible*'s lessons are about getting our behaviors in shape. Therefore, churches should be health clubs for becoming better versions of ourselves.

You've probably been to leadership seminars or read leadership books, right? Because you attended those seminars, is your life now perfect? I'll go one step further. Of all the leadership concepts you've learned about, which one have you perfected? Yeah, me too. Not one of them.

Some people present themselves as perfect or superior to others. However, this is not unique to churches. People across the globe exhibit this behavior. When it involves churchgoers or people who claim to be spiritual, regardless of whether they attend church or not, it does not help to attract others to the teachings of the *Bible*. I've worked in companies where people think they are superior to others, which made working there difficult. We cannot leave a workplace as easily as we can avoid a church. We have bills to pay and are tethered to producing an income.

People see this superiority complex as a form of hypocrisy. People run around spouting random verses, condemning others for bad behavior. All the while, they do not live perfectly. I've had top-level executives spout rules to me about how I need to follow company procedures. And then, minutes later, watch them violate those very rules. People see the church as full of hypocrites. I'll tell you right now: every one of us is a hypocrite at some point. Come on down to the church; we have room for one more.

Think of hypocrisy as the cholesterol of your blood. The idea is to work on lowering it. Saying, "I can't go to church because people there are sinners and hypocrites," is like saying, "I can't go to a health club because out-of-shape people go there." Health clubs are for getting healthy. Churches are supposed to be for helping people become better people.

## Misconception #8: Church and religion is about rituals that make people puppets (controlling people)

We touched on this in misconception #3. There is a difference between performing mindless rituals and creating effective habits. The *Bible* tells us to build habits through practice.

In the Book of Matthew, chapter 23, Verses 13 through 29 address rituals versus what it takes to follow the lessons of the *Bible*. Remember, in chapter eight, we learned how Paul was imprisoned for teaching the lessons of the *Bible* that he learned from Jesus.

In a public square, in front of a crowd of people, Jesus gets right in the face of the Pharisees. He goes on a tirade, a long, angry speech of criticism.

Jesus calls them out for focusing on the offerings, counting the gold and gifts, and using that money to build shrines and elaborate tombs and buy expensive spices that they carefully measure. Then, they neglect those whom they should be helping.

The Pharisees were supposed to be leading the churches and helping those in need. Jesus surrounded himself with people in need of help. He reformed a greedy tax collector, Matthew, and helped Mary of Magdala. Mary had demons, which included gambling, drinking, prostitution, and so forth. Jesus helped her turn her life around.

Churches were supposed to be about helping others. Many of the religious leaders of Jesus' time removed themselves from problematic people. They had a long list of people unworthy of their presence: tax collectors, Samaritans, drunks, prostitutes, etc. Their separatist mentality isolated them from the people who needed help the most.

The Pharisees were the so-called experts. Jesus and his students weren't authorized to help others. That was the job of the Pharisees, and they felt threatened. Yet they were avoiding those truly in need. They disliked Jesus because he associated with tax collectors,

Samaritans, drunks, and prostitutes, and he bypassed the self-imposed authority of the Pharisees to help others.

My early experience with the church mirrors what the Pharisees did thousands of years ago. We went; the service had a specific format, and we uttered the exact phrases each week while sitting, standing, and kneeling like a choreographed stage play. I'm pretty sure this is why so many people see religions as some cult full of puppets.

People show up, go through the steps, and then go back to doing whatever they usually do. There are churches that are addressing many of these challenges. Find one that focuses on helping people.

## Misconception #9: Money is the root of all evil.

The concept that "money is the root of all evil" never came from the *Bible*. Money is not the root of evil; the love *of money* is a root of all kinds of evil.

> *For the love of money is a root of all kinds of evil.*
> *Some people, eager for money, have wandered from*
> *the faith and pierced themselves with many griefs.*
> ~1 Timothy 6:10 (NIV)

This passage says, "a root of all kinds of evil." That's because a person's love for many things can lead to different forms of evil. If you love cookies and other sweets and eat them all the time in large quantities, you'll become obese. You're doing evil to your body.

Your love of cookies is a root of evil. The cookies aren't evil.

In 1 Timothy, chapter 6, verses 4 through 9 address envy, strife, malicious talk, evil suspicions, and constant friction between people of corrupt mind. The love of money drives things like temptation and harmful desires that plunge people into ruin and destruction.

## Misconception #10: The Bible tells us it's okay to take revenge.

The title of this section in the Book of Exodus, chapter 21, verses 12 through 36, is "Personal injuries." It's a long and detailed lesson. I will provide verses 12 through 27. Pull it up on your phone and look at verses 28 through 36 to see the balance of the lessons.

*Anyone who strikes a person with a fatal blow is to be put to death. However, if it is not done intentionally, but God lets it happen, they are to flee to a place I will designate. But if anyone schemes and kills someone deliberately, that person is to be taken from my altar and put to death.*

*Anyone who attacks their father or mother is to be put to death.*

*Anyone who kidnaps someone is to be put to death, whether the victim has been sold or is still in the kidnapper's possession.*

*Anyone who curses their father or mother is to be put to death.*

*If people quarrel and one person hits another with a stone or with their fist and the victim does not die but is confined to bed, the one who struck the blow will not be held liable if the other can get up and walk around outside with a staff; however, the guilty party must pay the injured person for any loss of time and see that the victim is completely healed.*

*Anyone who beats their male or female slave with a rod must be punished if the slave dies as a direct result, but they are not to be punished if the slave recovers after a day or two, since the slave is their property.*

*If people are fighting and hit a pregnant woman and she gives birth prematurely but there is no serious injury, the offender must be fined whatever the woman's husband demands and the court allows. But if there is serious injury, you are to take life for life, eye for eye, tooth for tooth, hand for hand, foot for foot, burn for burn, wound for wound, bruise for bruise.*

*An owner who hits a male or female slave in the eye and destroys it must let the slave go free to compensate for the eye. And an owner who knocks*

*out the tooth of a male or female slave must let the*
*slave go free to compensate for the tooth.*
~ Exodus 21:12-27 (NIV)

Here are just a few of the things this passage covers.

- ✓ When two people get into an argument, you cannot escalate it and physically harm the other person.
- ✓ You cannot physically harm someone who works for you as an indentured servant.
- ✓ Perhaps we should take acts of violence as seriously as they did. People would think twice about attacking or talking back to their parents.
- ✓ If you own dangerous animals like bulls, make sure they are contained so they do not harm someone. If they do, you are responsible for damages.
- ✓ If someone is doing construction, you must keep the area safe so that others will not be harmed. If they are, then you are responsible for damages.

Sounds exactly like the things we talk about today, doesn't it? Yes, it does.

In verses 23 through 27, there's language about a tooth for a tooth, an eye for an eye, a foot for a foot, a burn for a burn, a wound for a wound, and a bruise for a bruise. Does this lesson tell us that if a person injures us, we can seek retribution and revenge and do the same to them? No.

Exodus explains what "equal compensation" might look like for injury to others. If you have an indentured servant and you injure them, you must set them free. It's an analogy. Knock out a tooth; the tooth you must now give up is the debt they owe you—something of equal value.

The lesson even discusses compensation for lost wages and time. It's funny how we think the work issues we deal with today are somehow new.

## My advice to you, the reader.

It's always about context. As I have stated in all my books, I am not telling you what to think; I'm helping you think for yourself. Do not look at any single verse in the *Bible* and take what someone presents as reality—not even my interpretations. It's okay not to agree with anything I illustrate in my books. I welcome the discussion.

When you disagree, ask, did I hear it wrong? Did I misinterpret what they said? Most importantly, why did I not agree with it? Is it based on my beliefs or my experiences? It could simply be a different perspective.

Even if I still disagree with it, I must let it go. As the song in the movie *Frozen* tells us, "Let it go." If I do not let it go and get stuck on that one point, then I will miss the other lessons in the message that can benefit me.

No matter where you are, in a leadership seminar, any training, or a church service, there are things you will not agree with or understand. When it comes to *Bible* passages, instead of just reading a single verse, read as much of the chapter or chapters as you need to gain enough insight into what lesson is being presented.

Here is a list of questions you should ask...

- ✓ Who wrote it?
- ✓ To whom was it written?
- ✓ What was happening? (Example: Jonah Story)
- ✓ Why did they write it? In other words, for what purpose? What lesson or wisdom was the writer trying to pass on to them?
- ✓ What analogies and metaphors did they use to illustrate the lesson? Did they exaggerate or embellish to make a point?
- ✓ Which *Bible* version(s) might help me to understand the translations better? You can look at the difference between older and newer translations in the language. For example, KJV versus NKJV. The "N" stands for "New." It's the New King James Version. When I research, I look at one or more of these versions: KJV, NKJV, NIV, ESV, NLT, TPT, and MSG. Ensure you get permission to use quotes from any version of the *Bible*.

How about the concept of miracles? What do you think about "miracle" language in the *Bible*?

# CHAPTER ELEVEN

# I Believe In Miracles

Ming Wang was born in 1960 in China and grew up during the Chinese Cultural Revolution that took place from 1966 to 1976.

Ming comes from five generations of doctors. From an early age, he dreamed of following in their footsteps. This dream had many challenges that most of us will never face. During that cultural revolutionary period in the 1960s, schools were shut down.

Imagine the dream of becoming anything that requires an education, and you do not have access to schools. Ming Wang never gave up. Eventually, schools reopened, and he began to further his education. At the age of 21, in 1982, he arrived in the U.S. with $50 and a suit his mother bought him with what little savings she had.

At the age of 6, Ming witnessed his father help a family friend who was severely hurt and blinded. This experience determined which doctoral path Ming would choose. Ming graduated magna cume laude from Harvard Medical School and MIT and earned his Ph.D. in laser physics from the University of Maryland. From there, with the help of many others, he would invent and patent the amniotic membrane contact lens.

During Dr. Wang's journey to help people repair and restore their sight, a blind orphan named Kajal, a young girl from Calcutta, India entered Wang's world. Her stepmother intentionally blinded Kajal. This evil stepmother poured sulfuric acid into her eyes.

Kajal was brought to Dr. Wang's attention by a Christian social work group called Society of Underprivileged People. That organization had found her and sought medical treatments that might restore her sight.

Kajal's surgery would be Dr. Wang's first attempt to use the amniotic membrane contact lens to restore a person's vision. Wang's efforts to treat Kajal failed. He thought that curing her blindness would be a miracle. It turns out that not succeeding was also a miracle. In what way would this non-success be a miracle? We need to reframe our view of what constitutes a miracle.

The movie *Sight* is based on Wang's autobiography, "From Darkness to Sight." In the movie, they share how Kajal would help other children understand that having sight is a gift. We take so many things for granted, including our sight. It was a lesson about being grateful for something the children already had, not looking for happiness in things they did not possess. She did not have the gift of sight, yet she was joyful, happy, and lived a full life. Kajal eventually returned to India, went to college, and earned her master's degree.

Where do we find this lesson about not looking for happiness in some random material things, to not look to the future? but rather being satisfied with what you have and how that leads to contentment? In the *Bible*.

> *I know what it is to be in need, and I know what*
> *it is to have plenty. I have learned the secret of*
> *being content in any and every situation,*
> *whether well fed or hungry, whether living in*
> *plenty or in want. I can do all this through him*
> *who gives me strength.*
> ~ Philippians 4:12-13 (NIV)

Not being able to cure her blindness created the miracle of "her ability to teach the lesson of gratefulness in others." We forget to be grateful for the simple things we already have until we lose them. As Earl Nightengale says in his 1957 radio broadcast...

> *The problem is that our mind comes as standard*
> *equipment at birth. It's free. And things that are given*
> *to us for nothing, we place little value on. Things that*
> *we pay money for, we value.*

The fact that we have our sight, our hearing, all our limbs, and our health, we take all of these things for granted. That is, until we lose them. We place more value on material things.

Although not cured of her blindness, Kajal participated in and became a symbol for the Wang Foundation. Wang almost gave up his pursuit to cure blindness altogether after not restoring Kajal's sight. But dancing with her at the Wang Foundation's annual benefit, the EyeBall gala, in 2007, changed his perspective. She was the miracle that inspired Dr. Wang to continue and not give up. What if it had been another blind person, not Kajal, and that same inspiration never happened? What were the results of his continued efforts?

Maria Morari, a 15-year-old orphan from Moldova, Romania, was blind her entire life. After arriving in the United States, Dr. Wang surgically implanted the amniotic membrane contact lens into one of her eyes. That surgery was a success. Maria now had the gift of sight. She was the first person to have restored vision by surgically implanting the amniotic membrane contact lens. Imagine seeing yourself in a mirror for the first time at the age of 15. That's a miracle.

According to the official website, Drmingwang.com, all of these miracles have transpired.

> *As an eye surgeon in Nashville, TN, Dr. Wang has performed over 55,000 procedures, including on over 4,000 doctors. He has published over 100 papers, including one in the world-renowned journal Nature and 10 ophthalmic textbooks.*

> *The Wang Foundation for Sight Restoration, a 501c(3) non-profit charity founded by Dr. Wang, has helped patients from over 40 states in the U.S. and 55 countries worldwide, with all sight restoration surgeries performed free of charge.*

This story is filled with miracles. We need to see miracles from a different perspective, reframe how we look for them, and redefine what constitutes a miracle. Miracles are all around us. Because of some stories in the *Bible*, people think of miracles in terms of Jesus laying his hand on a person and "boom," they are instantly healed. "When I see something like that, I'll believe in miracles," they expound.

Because humans are different from any other species on earth and because universal principles apply to all of us, ones that are given to us through a First Cause, we can do miracles.

Dr. Wang's journey paints a very different picture of what represents a miracle. It is also a story about where he gets the gifts he has to accomplish these surgeries. You can find the details of his journey to faith on wangfoundation.com.

Like many people, Ming Wang's early life was not about religion in any way. His need to find the answer to why things happen in life led him to believe there is a First Cause behind everything he has accomplished. He says it's God.

In Philippians 4:13 it says, "I can do all this through him who gives me strength." It's done by enacting the universal principles of life. Have faith that it can be done, to believe. Take actions that begin and continue a progression. Sometimes, you will have success; sometimes, you will not. Along the way, you will gain insight. You will collaborate with someone or something. The five components in the BASIC Leadership blueprint's outer wheel are how life operates in general.

They illustrate the way the universal principles of life operate.

When a person says, "God performs miracles through us," this is what it means. The human ability to solve problems through science, which consists of universal laws from a universal First Cause, is how God performs miracles through us.

Dr. Wang had been living his life through science. Without the preceding chapters, where we addressed the word "God," reframing and changing our perspective, what would you have thought about the mindset that Dr. Wang has in terms of religion?

So many miracles have occurred because of his actions. The things you do every day can create little miracles. Those little miracles will only occur when a person acts in leadership. We never hear phrases like, "Hallelujah, that arsonist burned down three buildings. It's a miracle." Nothing that lacks integrity or that exists on the negative side of the leadership lifeline is representative of a miracle.

We have been told that God does things for us. This premise is misleading. The universe operates through universal principles and laws. These universal principles are provided to us, but we must live by and through them. This deeper understanding is what Dr. Wang realized during his search for why things happen in life.

Churches, pastors, preachers, and priests say things like, "Leave it in God's hands" or "It is in God's hands now," as if we should then do nothing. Everything I find within the lessons of the *Bible* tells us just the opposite.

Dozens of passages contain phrases such as "work of our hands" or "equip you with everything good for doing his will." Here are two examples.

*May the favor of the Lord our God rest on us;*
*establish the work of our hands for us—*
*yes, establish the work of our hands.*
~Psalm 90:17 (NIV)

When we act in leadership, we are aligning ourselves with the natural principles and universal laws that exist. This alignment gives us favor. These principles guide us, but we must do the work.

*Now may the God of peace, who through the blood*
*of the eternal covenant brought back from the*
*dead our Lord Jesus, that great Shepherd of the*
*sheep, equip you with everything good for doing his*
*will, and may he work in us what is pleasing to*
*him, through Jesus Christ, to whom be glory for ever*
*and ever. Amen.*
~Hebrews 13:20-21 (NIV)

Again, we must take action, "equip you with everything good for doing his will." This misconception that responsibility is not ours reminds me of the parable of The Farmer and the Preacher.

*A preacher was driving down a country road when*
*he came upon the most beautiful farm he'd ever*
*seen in his lifetime. He could only compare it to a*
*beautiful painting. The house was well maintained,*
*surrounded by a magnificent garden full of colorful*

*flowers. A perfect row of trees lined each side of the white gravel drive. The fields were beautifully tilled, and a healthy herd of fat dairy cattle grazed in the greenest pastures.*

*The site was so breathtaking that the preacher stopped to admire it. The preacher had been raised on a farm himself and knew a great farm when he saw one.*

*As he gazed upon this farm, he noticed the farmer on a tractor. When the farmer got closer, the preacher hailed him. The farmer stopped the tractor, walked over to the preacher, and smiled and said, "Hello!"*

*The preacher said to him, "My goodness, God has certainly blessed you with a magnificent farm."*

*The farmer paused, removed his cap, and, with humble eyes, looked around to examine his accomplishments. He then turned to the preacher and said, "Yes, He has, and we're grateful. But you should have seen this place when He had it all to Himself."*

Each one of us is a farmer. Our lives are the plots of ground given to us free and clear. If we're wise, we will also reap the abundant harvest. However, the planting is left strictly to us. "It's up to us to do it" is one of the many lessons the *Bible* teaches us.

We are to do "good works," not just any old work. We find this in the letters that Paul wrote to the Ephesians and to the Roman church.

*For we are God's handiwork, created in Christ Jesus
to do good works, which God prepared in advance
for us to do.*
~Ephesians 2:10 (NIV)

*And we know that in all things God works for the
good of those who love him, who have been
called according to his purpose.*
~Romans 8:28 (NIV)

When we do good works and do not give up, just like Dr. Ming Wang, we believe that when we keep going, we will have hope, we can prosper, and also accomplish miracles. These miracles do not have to be gigantic, life-altering things.

Do something nice for someone today without the expectation of anything in return. That simple act of kindness can have a domino effect in life. That person will feel good and do some little thing that eventually progresses into something big. We've seen this principle presented as "pay it forward."

There are countless people who have done something small that led to an incredible thing in the future—something they might never live to see. But because of that small gesture, something miraculous happened.

The *Bible* teaches the lessons of acting in leadership. Acting in leadership is done by following universal principles and laws. These principles and laws are by design and require a First Cause intelligence. They are the blueprint for how to live life.

# CHAPTER TWELVE

# What Is Our Purpose?

If I were to ask you, "What is your purpose in life?" how would you respond? Too often, we hear that we all have a purpose. I disagree with that statement. We do not have a single purpose; we can have many. Instilling the idea that anyone has a single purpose and then trying to find that singular thing would drive any person insane. Not to mention that the debates over who is right would be endless.

The stress and anxiety associated with identifying a singular purpose have been accelerated by mixing in the concept of how we all need to find our why. As if some singular why also exists, and a why is somehow different from a purpose. So, of course, due to my analytical nature, I researched the difference between purpose and why. What I found was a muddled-up mess of contradictions and disagreement.

- According to the Cambridge dictionary, a purpose is why you do something. Therefore, purpose and why are the same thing.
- According to the Oxford dictionary, purpose is "the reason for," which translates to "why."
- According to the Merriam-Webster dictionary, purpose is associated with an end result.
- Dictionary.com says purpose is both the reason, aka why, and the end result.

That's just the tip of the iceberg. When we look at all the people trying to sell us something to help us in business, they all have dozens of different explanations regarding the difference between purpose and why. If you can confuse someone, you can entice them to buy whatever you are offering as a solution to remove that confusion. It always seems to come right back to attaching everything to business. This attachment to business is not unexpected since we attempt to attach everything to business, just like we misguidedly attached leadership to doing business. What I found was a high level of complexity. The Loop of Optimal effectiveness, again, is in full play. So now what?

Simon Sinek provides some insight in his book *Start With Why*. Most people know what they do, most people are pretty good at knowing how to do something, but very few know why they do it.

First, as I stated at the beginning of this chapter, we mistakenly think we have only one purpose. We can have many, and some can change often and quickly. Second, why we do something ties directly with the benefits it provides, not only to ourselves, but to an entire society. Humans are benefit-driven. No benefit, no reason to do something. Third, we can have a purpose with an end result and a purpose that is continuous, a progression toward something.

Since we can have multiple purposes in life, and sometimes those can change, the question becomes, is there a purpose that is universal and does not change? A purpose that would apply to everyone equally and, when acted upon, would benefit the individual and society as a whole? The answer is yes.

In the previous chapter, we learned that Dr. Ming Wang, along with others, developed the amniotic membrane contact lens and created the procedures for the surgery that would restore sight for some people. When we ask ourselves "What is my purpose in life?" we tend to think in terms of what Dr. Wang accomplished. We compare what we have done in our lives to those types of accomplishments.

As odd as it sounds, the creation of the amniotic membrane contact lens and developing the procedures for the surgery, and restoring the sight of blind people, none of those things were Dr. Wang's purpose in life. Restoring sight to the blind was "an end result" of continually acting in leadership.

I did not write about Dr. Wang because he restored sight to some people. I wrote about him to illustrate what constitutes a miracle. That was the purpose of that chapter.

One of our primary purposes in life is to be in alignment with the universal principles and laws of how we behave, how we act, and how we conduct ourselves. The end result of Dr. Wang restoring people's sight is because he was in alignment with the teachings and lessons of the *Bible*. That's how he indirectly describes what happened.

In chapter nine, we learned to reframe language. The universal principles and laws came into existence from First Cause. The Bible uses the label of God. If God, aka First Cause, created universal principles and laws that apply to everyone, then we act in leadership to be in alignment. This is what it means to "do it all for the glory of God." We see this in the first Book of Corinthians, chapter 10, verse 31.

> So whether you eat or drink or whatever you do,
> do it all for the glory of God.
> ~1 Corinthians 10:31 (NIV)

Chapter ten of the first Book of Corinthians provides some detail on what not to do and warns against immoral behaviors. We glorify God by living the lessons taught in the *Bible*, we act in leadership. Just to be clear, acting in leadership is not all we do, but it is the premise of this book.

Dr Wang's beliefs, actions, progression toward a worthy ideal, use of insights, and collaboration with others to make it happen led to a miracle. Miracles are only derived from acting with integrity and existing on the positive side of the leadership lifeline.

In chapter eight, we looked at BASIC Leadership in the *Bible*. I align acting in leadership with one of many of God's callings to us. We know that there is a First Cause; the *Bible* uses the label God. We know that the universal principles and scientific laws that tell us when we are acting in leadership come from the initial creation.

If your task at hand was to deconstruct and then reconstruct, to reframe the following passage, what do you think it tells us in modern-day language?

> *His divine power has given us everything we need for a godly life through our knowledge of him who called us by his own glory and goodness. Through these he has given us his very great and precious promises, so that through them you may participate in the divine nature, having escaped the corruption in the world caused by evil desires.*
>
> *For this very reason, make every effort to add to your faith goodness; and to goodness, knowledge; and to knowledge, self-control; and to self-control, perseverance; and to perseverance, godliness; and to godliness, mutual affection; and to mutual affection, love. For if you possess these qualities in increasing measure, they will keep you from being ineffective and unproductive in your knowledge of our Lord Jesus Christ. But whoever does not have them is nearsighted and blind, forgetting that they have been cleansed from their past sins.*
>
> *Therefore, my brothers and sisters, make every effort to confirm your calling and election. For if*

*you do these things, you will never stumble,*
~2 Peter 1:3-10 (NIV)

The title of this passage is "Confirming One's Calling and Election." A calling or election is a purpose. Do you believe that Dr. Ming Wang made every effort in good faith, gained insight through knowledge, persevered, and did it out of love? Or do you think anything Dr. Wang did was born out of evil desire?

When we are in alignment with the universal principles and laws of how we behave, how we act, and how we conduct ourselves, we are in alignment with God's word, with the universal principles and laws came into existence from First Cause.

The creation of the amniotic membrane contact lens, the development of the surgery procedures, and the restoration of the sight of blind people were the end results of being in alignment with God's word, the teachings, and the lessons of the *Bible*.

One of our purposes, and I would argue a primary one, is to be in alignment with God's word. We behave, we act, and we conduct ourselves according to the lessons of acting in leadership. The *Bible* provides us with the blueprint for doing so. If the *Bible* teaches acting in leadership, then our purpose is to glorify God by acting in leadership.

What we do is act in leadership. How we do it is defined by the BASIC Leadership blueprint. The why, our reason, is simple. We do this because, when everyone acts in leadership, the world will become a better place.

When no agreed-upon moral standards exist, a society decays and eventually self-destructs. This is a universal truth, whether at the family level, community, nation, or globally. No one is arguing against this. Acting in leadership should be a primary purpose for everyone. The *Bible* teaches acting in leadership.

leadership.

# CHAPTER THIRTEEN

# Visions, Revelations, and Insight

One of the many lessons taught today is that a leader has vision; leaders are visionaries.

The word "vision" appears over 100 times in the *Bible*. A vision is the ability to think about or plan the future with imagination; a thought, concept, or object formed by the imagination; or a manifestation to the senses of something immaterial.

When we can physically touch something, we call it tangible. When we cannot, we say it is intangible. We cannot touch a vision. It is intangible, immaterial.

A vision can also be called a revelation. A revelation is an uncovering, a bringing to light of that which had been previously wholly hidden or only obscurely seen. When we gain insight, we uncover something obscure or hidden. We now understand something previously unknown.

We can envision how something might happen or come to be. According to modern-day leadership lessons, leaders are supposed to possess the attribute of being a visionary. Why does it seem so odd when we read about it in the *Bible*?

> *Write down the revelation*
> *and make it plain on tablets*
> *so that a herald may run with it.*
> ~Habakkuk 2:2 (NIV)

Let's look at this passage from a business standpoint. CEOs are supposed to be the visionaries of the organization. The CEO of a company wasn't sure what direction the organization should take. He or she thought about it for a bit, then had a revelation, an idea. They had a vision, wrote it down, and gave it to their executive team, their heralds, so they could pass it on to the rest of the organization.

The revelation, the vision brought to light in the Book of Habakkuk, Chapter 2, verse 2, shown above, were attributes associated with acting in leadership. That passage tells us not to steal and not to take advantage of others, both attributes of acting in leadership.

At some point, we have a revelation that these behaviors are bad, aka evil. They either lack integrity or fall on the negative side of the leadership lifeline, or both. According to PsychologyToday.com,

> *Alone among animals, humans have access to an*
> *immediate, first-hand emotional perception of the*

*"wrongness" of actions or agency of the self,
experienced as a sense of guilt or shame. We are
inherently wired to have a feeling of guilt when we
imagine that our actions have hurt someone. Studies
show that children express guilty feelings by the age
of 3, before they are capable of any sophisticated
moral reasoning.*

These attributes apply to everyone, not just people at
or near the top of any hierarchy. These acting in
leadership attributes are universal principles and laws
created by a First Cause, illustrated to us through biology
in the form of guilt and shame.

At some point, we all have the revelation, the vision,
the insight into what is right or wrong, good or evil,
moral or immoral. Let's look at another verse that talks
about vision.

*I was in the city of Joppa praying, and in a trance I
saw a vision. I saw something like a large sheet
being let down from heaven by its four corners, and
it came down to where I was.*
~Acts 11:5 (NIV)

Luke, an evangelist, wrote the Book of Acts. In this
book, Luke provides us with historical accounts of the
interactions between people sharing the lessons Jesus
taught. Two of those people were Peter and Paul. Peter
was one of the original twelve disciples of Jesus, and
Paul was a close companion of Luke.

In chapter 11, Luke describes how Peter was explaining his actions to Paul. Peter had been teaching the lessons of Jesus to Gentiles. Doing so in those times would be like someone in 1941 wanting to teach black men to be fighter pilots in World War II.

Based on real-life events, the movie *The Tuskegee Airmen* illustrates the same type of battle being fought. Racists said, "You can't teach black people to be fighter pilots; that's only for whites. They are unworthy and incapable." Paul opposed Peter and told Peter that he couldn't teach Gentiles those things; that's only for Jewish people. Gentiles are unworthy and incapable of understanding. History teaches us the same lessons over and over again.

Peter had a vision, a revelation, that these lessons should apply to everyone. This is very similar to today's misguided approach of saying that leadership is for those at the top of hierarchies.

Next, in chapter 16 in the Book of Jeremiah provides the lesson that not all visions are good visions.

> *Do not listen to what the prophets are prophesying to you;*
> *they fill you with false hopes.*
> *They speak visions from their own minds,*
> *not from the mouth of the LORD.*
> ~Jeremiah 23:16 (NIV)

Just because you had some thought or concept formed by your imagination does not mean you should act on it. You had this vision that if you robbed a bank, it would solve all your problems. That's a vision from your own mind and not a universal principle for acting in leadership. It's false hope and will likely not turn out so well.

In verse 12, just before verse 16, we see this...

> *Therefore their path will become slippery;*
> *they will be banished to darkness*
> *and there they will fall.*
> *I will bring disaster on them*
> *in the year they are punished,"*
> *declares the LORD.*
> ~Jeremiah 23:12 (NIV)

Criminals go down slippery paths. A person who robs a bank will likely go to jail. They bring it upon themselves. They will be banished to a small, dingy, cold, dark prison cell. Why? Because it is wrong. Any form of not acting in leadership can have consequences. In the story of Jonah and the Whale, we learn that we can be imprisoned in a dark pit of guilt or shame.

When I witness someone rob a bank, and then I say to the person next to me, "They're probably going to end up in Jail," that's prophesying. I saw their possible future. If you witness an entire city turning into a dumpster fire like in the Jonah and the Whale story, and you say, "This isn't going to end well," that's no different than what a prophet might be able to logically conclude 2,000 years ago.

These are stories presented as parables, using analogies and metaphors. Some parts are true, and other parts are embellished for effect. If there are universal principles that govern our behavior, just like there are universal laws that govern things like gravity and electricity, violating them has consequences.

Throw a rock as hard as you can straight up into the air, and then standing there while it drops can have consequences. You can't do that and expect the rock not to follow the law of gravity. Likewise, you cannot violate the universal principles of good and bad behavior and not expect consequences eventually.

Throw a rock straight up into the air and stand there. It will not always hit you when it comes back down. But do it enough times, and the odds of something bad happening will increase dramatically.

Each morning, every one of us envisions what our day will look like. Some have a vision of a positive day with positive outcomes. Some see a negative day with negative outcomes. How did you envision your day when you woke up this morning? Were your thoughts negatively based simply because of the day of the week, Monday? Tell me what thoughts you have as you begin each day, and I will have a revelation of how your day will go and end. Your life becomes what you think about.

Some people understood the vision and revelation connection thousands of years ago. They wrote stories about actual events to illustrate these universal principles. If you are following the principles of acting in leadership, then you are already following the lessons taught in the *Bible*.

# CHAPTER FOURTEEN

# Progression or Escalation? Positive or Negative?

## *Escalation*

So much of what we do in today's world is not a progression but rather an escalation. Progressing toward a worthy ideal is significantly different than escalation. Some of the language we use today did not exist in the *Bible*. We already learned this in an earlier chapter. Language continues to expand over time.

The word escalation did not become popular until the 1930s, but it helps us understand what we mean when distinguishing between progression and escalation.

Escalation is about taking things to an excessive level. For example, when eating more than is necessary to be healthy, a person becomes overweight or obese. The

*Bible* illustrates escalation in the context of food with the word gluttony.

Gluttony is called an evil thing. Evil means bad. We are escalating something to a higher level than is healthy for us. Similarly, the word greed is used to address how we escalate when it comes to money and material things. In chapter 7, I used the passage from the Book of Proverbs to talk about envy. This passage also illustrates the lesson of gluttony and how gluttony is bad.

> *Do not join those who drink too much wine*
> *or gorge themselves on meat,*
> *for drunkards and gluttons become poor,*
> *and drowsiness clothes them in rags.*
> ~Proverbs 23:20-21 (NIV)

> *It is not good to eat too much honey,*
> *nor is it honorable to search out matters that are*
> *too deep.*
> *Like a city whose walls are broken through*
> *is a person who lacks self-control.*
> ~ Proverbs 25:27-28 (NIV)

Proverbs 25:27-28 is an analogy of how our self-control is like a city wall. Lack of self-control against escalation is like breaking your personal city wall and allowing gluttony and greed to enter unchecked.

In the Book of Galatians, chapter 5, verses 22 through 24, we see self-control mentioned again.

> *But the fruit of the Spirit is love, joy,*
> *peace, forbearance, kindness, goodness,*

*faithfulness, gentleness and self-control. Against such things there is no law. Those who belong to Christ Jesus have crucified the flesh with its passions and desires.*

~ Galatians 5:22–24 (NIV)

In chapter nine, we learned that Paul wrote the letters to the Philippians while in prison. The *Bible* contains around 58 verses that address self-control and just as many verses and stories on how to develop it.

We think the concept of a progression includes anything. It does not. One way to determine if a person is escalating is that it induces a much higher level of anxiety, worry, and stress than a natural progression. Self-control is the antidote for escalation.

Being in debt causes anxiety, worry, and stress. You've escalated your spending. When you become overweight, it is because you have escalated your food intake and have not gotten enough exercise. We think escalation happens in one direction. That is a flawed assumption to make.

We should get constant, moderate exercise and the proper amount of rest. When we do not participate in continuous, moderate exercise, we become lazy. Lazy is an escalation of relaxation. Relaxation is a good thing unless we escalate it. We increase our food intake and the time spent being sedentary, which together make us extremely unhealthy.

*Lazy hands make for poverty,*

*but diligent hands bring wealth.*
~Proverbs 10:4 (NIV)

When we see the words "poverty" and "wealth," we constantly think in terms of money. You can experience poverty in many ways, including your health and relationships. When we escalate on the positive side of the leadership lifeline, it then shifts from something positive to something negative. For instance, relaxation is good. But too much of it isn't good. Having a plan and taking action on things is good. Always being active, and push, push, push, then it becomes unhealthy.

So-called leadership experts tell us that leaders must be extraordinary, causing anxiety, worry, and stress. Misguided advice is driving everybody to think they have to be extraordinary to be a leader. This is in direct contrast to acting in leadership.

Do not mistake escalation for a natural progression.

## Leadership Lifeline

When it comes to the leadership lifeline, we will encounter concepts that require a bit more insight to determine whether they are positive or negative. We will look at three examples: guilt, shame, and doubt.

First, there is no source anywhere, including the *Bible,* that says the things that land on the negative side of the lifeline will completely go away. The fact that we can't permanently fix everything is also true of things that do not pass through the integrity hub. We cannot completely wipe them out. We addressed this in chapter

10, Bible Misconceptions. Challenges in life will never go away. What we can do is understand how these challenges, obstacles, and adverse situations impact our lives and take the necessary actions to minimize them.

We intrinsically know that certain things exist only on the positive side of the leadership lifeline. Trust would be one of those things. Trust binds a society together. It is one of the foundational principles for cooperation, social harmony, reduced conflict, and increased stability, to name a few. Act in a manner that will not pass the integrity test or act in a manner that lands on the negative side of the leadership lifeline, and trust is reduced. Lie to someone, and they will trust you less.

There are also some things that exist only on the negative side of the leadership lifeline. Galatians, chapter 5, verses 19 through 21, provides us a list of things we know for sure that fall on the negative side.

> *The acts of the flesh are obvious: sexual*
> *immorality, impurity and debauchery; idolatry and*
> *witchcraft; hatred, discord, jealousy, fits of rage,*
> *selfish ambition, dissensions, factions and envy;*
> *drunkenness, orgies, and the like. I warn you, as I*
> *did before, that those who live like this will not*
> *inherit the kingdom of God.*
> ~Galatians 5:19-21 (NIV)

Two items in that list need some context. These are faction and dissensions. A faction is a small, organized dissenting group within a larger one. The context we need to have regarding the *Bible* is that in this passage, faction and dissension refer to someone who thinks that things like hatred are okay. They are in opposition to the lessons of acting in leadership.

Next, when something exists only on one side of the leadership lifeline, a contrasting component exists on the other side. Everything has a balance, a yin and yang. Two elements that contrast each other are responsibility and blame. In modern times, we say leaders take responsibility. When we accept responsibility for what we have done, it falls on the positive side.

> *Whoever conceals their sins does not prosper,*
>   *but the one who confesses and renounces them*
> *finds mercy.*
>       ~Proverbs 28:13 (NIV)

This passage is about taking responsibility for our own actions. When we see the word "confess," we tend to associate it with religion or criminals. Confession means admitting something. We miss that the lesson is for everyone, not just for people who attend church and participate in the ritual of going into a little booth and telling things to a priest.

This lesson illustrates how when a person screws up and then takes responsibility, they feel relieved. That's what "finding mercy" refers to. When we do something wrong, guilt sets in, we take responsibility, and the weight of guilt is lifted; we find mercy and get relief from guilt. The lesson does not end there. To "renounce it" means we will not repeat that same thing. Renounce means to abandon, to stop doing that thing.

In contrast to responsibility, we have blame. Blame exists on the negative side.

> *The man said, "The woman you put here with me—*
> *she gave me some fruit from the tree, and I ate it."*
>
> *Then the Lord God said to the woman, "What is this*
> *you have done?"*
>
> *The woman said, "The serpent deceived me, and I*
> *ate."*
>
> ~Genesis 3:12-13 (NIV)

The Book of Genesis addresses blaming others. Adam and Eve are told not to eat from the Tree of Knowledge. When they do, Adam blames Eve, and Eve blames the snake. It's one of the first lessons in the *Bible*.

Beyond the obvious things that either exist only on the positive side or the negative side, we will encounter concepts that appear contradictory or that create a struggle to determine on which side they might exist. To make that determination, we need context, just like we did for dissension and faction. We'll dig into guilt, shame, and doubt to add context.

Guilt is addressed around 180 times in the *Bible*. In chapter five, we saw a powerful example of how guilt exists on the positive side of the leadership lifeline: the story of Jonah and the Whale. Guilt is a built-in mechanism that lets us know when something we have done or thought violates the integrity hub or exists on the negative side of the leadership lifeline. We can be overcome with guilt when we steal, lie, cheat, etc.

If guilt is a universal principle, part of universal mechanisms for detecting when a person has acted wrongly, why do some people not feel guilty? Great question. When you run electricity through your home, and one of the outlets does not work, is that because the universal laws that govern how electricity acts have changed? No. There is an issue with the wiring. Some people have a wiring issue that causes the universal laws associated with guilt to not work. Or they learn to override them. We can intentionally bypass electrical systems in our homes, but that does not change the universal laws that govern electricity.

Guilt is a universal principle, an emotional law that detects when we have done something bad, wrong, or immoral. Things like do not murder, steal, or lie are universal laws. We know this because they cause guilt, which activates an internal emotion created by a universal First Cause.

We can even feel guilty just thinking about doing something immoral, like cheating, lying, or stealing. We get nervous, sweaty, etc. These are all mechanisms of universal laws built in through the First Cause. We see this "thinking about it" principle in Matthew 5:27-29

> You have heard that it was said, "You shall not commit adultery." But I tell you that anyone who looks at a woman lustfully has already committed adultery with her in his heart. If your right eye

*causes you to stumble, gouge it out and throw it away. It is better for you to lose one part of your body than for your whole body to be thrown into hell.*

~Matthew 5:27-29 (NIV)

It's an analogy. We know that thinking about it and lusting in our minds can lead to the actual act of doing it. It is not a guarantee, but it can lead to it. We give power to analogies by providing imagery that is hard to forget. One eye represents bad thoughts, and the other represents good ones. Gouge out those evil thoughts, and you will see more clearly. No one is telling you to literally gouge an eye out.

We do not want to feel guilty, so we act rightly to avoid the discomfort. Hebrews 10:22 refers to a person's transition, the beginning of a progression, from thoughts and actions that cause us to feel guilty.

*let us draw near to God with a sincere heart and with the full assurance that faith brings, having our hearts sprinkled to cleanse us from a guilty conscience and having our bodies washed with pure water.*

~ Hebrews 10:22 (NIV)

We have a guilty conscience because we did not act in leadership. Guilt of this type forces us to change. In this instance, we see how guilt is a good thing. It exists on the positive side of the leadership lifeline.

However, guilt is a bad thing when someone uses guilt to get you to do something, especially something that lacks integrity or lands on the negative side of the leadership lifeline. Searching the *Bible* for guilt in terms of guilting people into doing something bad proves very challenging.

In modern times, we call it "guilt-tripping." That language is not going to show up in the *Bible*. We have to connect the dots. Guilt-tripping is a form of manipulation. The person doing the guilt-tripping desires an outcome that benefits themself. People manipulate others using guilt to further themselves in life. That is called "selfish-ambition," also another form of escalation.

> *Do nothing out of selfish ambition or vain*
> *conceit. Rather, in humility value others above*
> *yourselves, not looking to your own interests but*
> *each of you to the interests of the others.*
> ~ Philippians 2:3-4 (NIV)

To be ambitious is not wrong. Selfish-ambition that includes manipulating others is wrong. We guilt-trip someone through manipulation to fulfill our selfish ambitions, whether for authority, money, material things, or even for amusement. Yes, we even guilt people into doing stupid things so we can laugh at them.

Guilt can exist on both sides of the leadership lifeline. Let's look at shame, another concept that can be found on both sides, positive and negative.

When we feel shame, it's another way to say guilt. When we feel ashamed of ourselves, it's nature's way of letting us know we did something unleaderly. When we shame others into doing something, it's a bad thing.

Next, what would we discover when we look at the concept of doubt? Which side of the leadership lifeline would you say it falls on? Positive? Negative? Both? Where would we find the lessons about doubt in the *Bible*? We need to connect the dots.

When we teach acting in leadership today, we say, "Encountering challenges strengthens us." When we overcome any challenge, we gain confidence that we can prevail when we encounter another similar challenge.

Even when we do not overcome that challenge, and it doesn't kill us, we look back and say, "That wasn't as bad as I thought it was." We utter the phrase, "What doesn't kill us makes us stronger."

Having doubts is a challenge we must overcome. It's okay to have doubts, but overcoming them makes us stronger. Stronger how? It strengthens our beliefs. Doubt means a feeling of uncertainty or lack of conviction. A lack of conviction means a person has no strong faith or belief in something. Overcoming our doubts builds confidence and belief in ourselves.

When someone says, "You're such a doubting Thomas," that comes from the *Bible*, the Book of John, chapter 20, verses 24 through 29.

*Now Thomas (also known as Didymus), one of the
Twelve, was not with the disciples when Jesus
came. So the other disciples told him, "We have
seen the Lord!"*

*But he said to them, "Unless I see the nail marks in
his hands and put my finger where the nails were,
and put my hand into his side, I will not believe."*

*A week later his disciples were in the house again,
and Thomas was with them. Though the doors were
locked, Jesus came and stood among them and
said, "Peace be with you!" Then he said to
Thomas, "Put your finger here; see my hands. Reach
out your hand and put it into my side. Stop doubting
and believe."*

*Thomas said to him, "My Lord and my God!"*

*Then Jesus told him, "Because you have seen me,
you have believed; blessed are those who have not
seen and yet have believed."*
~John 20:24-29 (NIV)

This passage tells us that it is okay to doubt. We all
have doubts. Overcoming our doubts makes us stronger.
In this case, it exists on the positive side of the
leadership lifeline.

But when does doubt land on the negative side?
Doubt is the fear of uncertainty. Fear is also both

negative and positive. Fear in the right circumstances keeps us safe. Fear that paralyzes us is unhealthy. That's why we say we must face our fears and overcome them. When doubt keeps you from taking action or from progressing, it exists on the negative side.

> *Examine yourselves to see whether you are in the faith; test yourselves. Do you not realize that Christ Jesus is in you—unless, of course, you fail the test?*
> ~2 Corinthians 13:5 (NIV)

Remember, from chapters eight and nine, faith and belief have the same definition.

- ➢ Belief: Trust, faith, or confidence in someone or something.
- ➢ Faith: Complete trust or confidence in someone or something.

We have to find out why we have those doubts. When we take action to face those doubts, just like our fears, we either confirm or change our current beliefs. Then we can move on. We are no longer paralyzed.

These escalation and leadership lifeline examples should suffice to help you analyze other concepts that seem a bit fuzzy or unclear. Next, is there such a thing as truth?

# CHAPTER FIFTEEN

# Your Truth, My Truth, and Scientific Truth

If a person were to say, "There is no truth," would that be true? It cannot be true if there are no truths. Kind of a mind scramble, huh?

There's a saying, "There are three truths: your truth, my truth, and the truth." This common saying highlights the potential for multiple interpretations of reality. Those interpretations are based on our individual experiences, while acknowledging the existence of an objective truth.

We know there are objective truths. Objective truth refers to a fact or reality that exists independently of personal beliefs or opinions, meaning it's true regardless of what anyone thinks or feels about it.

$1 + 1 = 2$ is true; therefore, it is a truthful statement. It is scientifically proven. The planets in our solar system orbit around our sun is also true; therefore, it is a truthful statement. We know these things to be truthful through science. Objective truths exist and are based on scientific evidence and facts.

The Earth is flat is someone's truth. Some people believe this, or at least claim to believe it. We know it to be false through science. At one point, many people thought the Earth was flat. It took hundreds of years to arrive at a "scientifically proven truth."

In 1543, Nicolaus Copernicus detailed his theory of the universe in which the Earth and other planets rotated around the Sun. People referred to Copernicus as radical. Acceptance of his idea by society required a long-term fight, taking more than a century. Now, we know the scientific truth about our solar system.

Since the last Book of the *Bible* was written nineteen centuries ago, and even more so for several centuries since the books have been translated into English, people have questioned pretty much everything presented in the *Bible*.

What do we now know scientifically about anger? Science tells us that getting angry releases the chemicals cortisol and adrenaline into our bodies. High levels of cortisol and adrenaline can damage our cells. Therefore, getting angry often and staying angry, especially at high levels, is bad. It's a foundational principle, a universal scientific law based on biology, not some off-the-wall theory.

It wasn't until the 1950s, through the research of Philip Hench, Edward Kendall, and Tadeus Reichstein, that we fully understood the effects of cortisol. That's not all that long ago, folks.

In chapter six, we began our lessons on acting in leadership by using the Book of Matthew, chapter 5, to address anger. Anger releases cortisol and adrenaline into our bodies. Too much cortisol can damage our cells; this cellular damage is based on scientific evidence.

> *You have heard that it was said to the people long ago, "You shall not murder, and anyone who murders will be subject to judgment." But I tell you that anyone who is angry with a brother or sister will be subject to judgment. Again, anyone who says to a brother or sister, "Raca," is answerable to the court. And anyone who says, "You fool!" will be in danger of the fire of hell.*
> ~Matthew 5:21-22 (NIV)

The title of this passage in the Book of Matthew is "Murder." Murder is addressed in one of the Ten Commandments. That lesson is obvious. Don't commit murder; you'll be subject to the courts. We tend to overlook the second lesson. If you get angry, you will also be subject to judgment. When we rephrase this passage, the lesson about anger becomes very apparent.

> *We've known murder is wrong for a very long time. But let me tell you something else: anger also has consequences. You will be punished if you do not keep it under control.*

A judgment is a formal decision by a court or a misfortune viewed as divine punishment. Get angry often and remain angry for long periods of time, especially at excessive levels, and your body has a built-in punishment mechanism. Cortisol and adrenaline get dumped into your body and damage your cells. Not only that, but anger can escalate to really bad things like murder. Anger has consequences, some obvious and some hidden under the surface.

Have you ever been told not to go to bed angry? Why? Where did that come from? It's in the Book of Ephesians, chapter 4, verse 26. We cannot get a good night's rest when we are angry. Whatever angers us is causing anxiety, worry, and stress, which keeps us awake.

> In your anger do not sin: Do not let the sun go down while you are still angry, and do not give the devil a foothold.
> ~Ephesians 4:26-27 (NIV)

Remember, Paul wrote letters to the Ephesians while he was in prison. Would he get any sleep if he stewed in anger over imprisonment? No. Who benefits if Paul does not get sleep? Certainly not Paul. It's a lesson he learned from Jesus.

In Matthew 5:25, the statement, "But I tell you that anyone who is angry with a brother or sister will be subject to judgment," is a scientifically proven truth. The language simply differs slightly from how we might present this lesson in modern times. The court passing judgment and imposing the penalty for anger exists in nature and the universe. Think of it as a universal principle, a universal law.

If the universe has built-in universal principles and natural laws that apply to everyone, and we use cognitive reframing to change our perspective on the label God, as we did in chapter nine, it all begins to make sense. If someone were to present this lesson on anger and say, "I'm speaking God's truth," they are talking about universal principles and natural laws by design from First Cause, and these laws apply to everyone

Jesus was a real person. He taught universal lessons from a First Cause, also referred to as God. In the Book of John, chapter 8, Jesus gives another TED Talk. This time, he also answers questions from the audience. Here is what he says.

> *To the Jews who had believed him, Jesus said, "If you hold to my teaching, you are really my disciples. Then you will know the truth, and the truth will set you free."*
> ~John 8:31-32 (NIV)

Not getting angry will set you free from many things. Free from internal chemicals that damage our bodies. Free from escalating to committing heinous acts such as murder due to raging anger. Free from lying awake all night, not getting any rest.

*All your words are true;*
*all your righteous laws are eternal.*
~Psalm 119:160 (NIV)

The format for the Book of Psalms is similar to the Book of Proverbs. It's poetic prose, short, simple lines that all connect together with details that provide the context of multiple lessons. Chapter 119 talks about all the stupid things we humans do to ourselves and each other. The stupid things we do are not attributes of acting in leadership.

Modern-day leadership lessons address anger. Leaders do not get angry; they remain calm. When a person is calm, they can think more clearly, make rational decisions, and innovate. The connection between the calmness of a person's mind and a person's ability to think more clearly is also scientifically proven. We'll talk more about that later.

Multiple scientifically proven natural laws regarding the consequences of anger exist. The *Bible* discusses all these different facets throughout the 66 books. Yes, there is your truth and my truth. The truths we should live by are the scientifically proven truths of the universal principles and natural laws put into place by First Cause. Those natural laws apply to everyone. The *Bible* teaches lessons that align with these universal principles and laws. They are eternal.

# CHAPTER SIXTEEN

# Meditation,
# Affirmations, and
# Prayer

In the previous chapter, I stated that when a person is calm, they can think more clearly, make rational decisions, and innovate. This foundational principle and universal law has been proven scientifically.

Meditation is a method taught for clearing our minds. As we see in the Book of Matthew, meditation is a theme of prayer.

> *But when you pray, go into your room, close the door and pray to your Father, who is unseen. Then your Father, who sees what is done in secret, will reward you. And when you pray, do not keep on babbling like pagans, for they think they will be*

*heard because of their many words.*
~Matthew 6:6-7 (NIV)

Methods for meditation require a person to go somewhere quiet and clear all the chatter in their heads. Jesus taught his disciples to meditate; he called it prayer.

Next, what is one method for creating a positive mindset? It's affirmations. Using affirmations is also one of the themes of prayer. Affirmations are positive statements that help you deal with negative feelings, thoughts, and situations. Research shows positive thinking can rewire your brain, changing how you view things.

The Book of Joshua, chapter 1, verse 8 tells us to meditate using *Bible* verses as affirmations.

*Keep this Book of the Law always on your*
*lips; meditate on it day and night, so that you may*
*be careful to do everything written in it. Then you*
*will be prosperous and successful.*
~Joshua 1:8 (NIV)

Every word we speak and every thought we have shapes our reality. Without realizing it, we are programming our minds to accept those outcomes, whether negative or positive. Every person has the ability to rewire their mind.

Our ability to remove doubt from our mind using affirmations is illustrated in the Book of Mark, chapter 11, "The Lesson of the Withered Fig Tree."

> *So Jesus answered and said to them, "Have faith in God. For assuredly, I say to you, whoever says to this mountain, 'Be removed and be cast into the sea,' and does not doubt in his heart, but believes that those things he says will be done, he will have whatever he says. Therefore I say to you, whatever things you ask when you pray, believe that you receive them, and you will have them.*
> ~Mark 11:22-24 (NKJV)

"I am calm," "I am a solutions person," and "I am content with what I have" are all affirmation statements. When you read modern-day teachings on how affirmations work, this passage looks like it came from a current-day leadership seminar. Let's reframe the above passage, Mark 11:22-24, into modern-day language.

> *To believe differently about yourself, meditate using affirmations to change how you see yourself. This will remove your doubts and change your beliefs about yourself. This scientifically proven method can transform negative beliefs into positive beliefs. If you believe this will work, then it will. This method is so powerful that it could remove and toss mountains of harmful beliefs into the sea.*

We speak words of defeat and limitation without realizing that we are programming our minds to accept those outcomes. If someone constantly says, "I'm not good enough," "I always fail," or "Nothing ever works out for me," they are training their mind to look for evidence to support those statements. Their actions will follow their thoughts and words. This rewiring of our brains is the law of attraction at work.

This universal law works in both directions, negative and positive. Prayers and affirmations such as "I am blessed" or "I am capable" drive us to look for evidence to support those statements.

However, because we use affirmations, it does not mean we can become whatever we want. A full-grown adult who is 5' 2" tall cannot affirm themselves into becoming an NBA basketball superstar. However, I have seen a person of this height kick the butt of a six-foot tall person in a game of one on one. The 5' 2" person believed they could become really good at basketball, so they took action to do so.

Today, we talk in terms of "mindset." A person who speaks positively about themselves, both in thought and spoken words, will see a non-success as something positive. That's a positive mindset. It is an opportunity to gain insight into what did not work and look for an alternate option. A positive attitude drives a person to continue to take more action. They see possibilities instead of limitations.

A person who speaks negatively about themselves, both in thought and spoken words, will see a non-success as something negative. They will see it as an obstacle that cannot be overcome. They see limitations instead of possibilities.

Psychology and neuroscience back up these truths. Our brains react just like our muscles. Whatever we think and say strengthens our beliefs, whether negative or positive. We're exercising our minds.

In chapter seven, we read an example of having a positive attitude in the Book of Proverbs, chapter 17, verse 22.

> *A cheerful heart is good medicine,*
> *but a crushed spirit dries up the bones.*
> ~Proverbs 17:22 (NIV)

Because repetition is how we learn and remember things, we find this lesson again in chapter 18 of the Book of Proverbs.

> *From the fruit of their mouth a person's stomach is*
> *filled; with the harvest of their lips they are*
> *satisfied.*
> *The tongue has the power of life and death,*
> *and those who love it will eat its fruit.*
> ~Proverbs 18:20-21 (NIV)

When we see the words "life" and "death," we tend to think in literal terms. What kind of life does a person live when they constantly have negative thoughts? Do they have a very fruitful life? No. Do they yield a satisfying harvest? No.

People with a positive outlook, those who see all things as possible, are truly living. Those with a negative outlook, those who see no possibilities, are not living. This is an analogy using hyperbole. Hyperbole means exaggerated statements or claims that are not meant to be taken literally. Life and death are hyperbole.

Positive affirmations are "life-giving" words and statements that encourage one to live a fruitful life and yield a harvest. We're gaining insight on how to view the language used in the English translations.

I researched the different types of prayer. Each has a specific purpose and objective.

- Petition: asking for something for ourselves (speaking positive things about ourselves)
- Intercession: asking for something for others (speaking positive things about others)
- Praise: recognizing the greatness of God (the power of universal laws)
- Confession: admitting our sins (taking responsibility for our actions)
- Peace of mind: quieting our thoughts to hear and see clearly
- Affirmations: reinforcing things that are good, positive, and helpful

The words "pray" or "prayer" are used approximately 121 times in the English translations of the *Bible*. Somehow, people think that praying is all about religion and that they have to be religious to pray. After gaining insight, we know that when a person is meditating and using affirmations, they are practicing forms of prayer. Modern-day leadership lessons teach us to calm our minds and think in positive terms.

Each of the above six types of prayer addresses a modern-day leadership principle. We need context to understand each type's purpose and objective.

For instance, Petition: asking for something for ourselves is not about acquiring wealth or material things. Similar to affirmations, petition is a form of rewiring our brains to address things like hate, revenge, and ill-will toward others.

One of the first prayers Jesus taught his twelve disciples is the Our Father Prayer.

*This, then, is how you should pray:*

*"Our Father in heaven,*
*hallowed be your name,*
*your kingdom come,*
*your will be done,*
  *on earth as it is in heaven.*
*Give us today our daily bread.*
 *And forgive us our debts,*
  *as we also have forgiven our debtors.*
*And lead us not into temptation,*
  *but deliver us from the evil one."*
            ~Matthew 6:9-13 (NIV)

We forgive those who trespass against us. What does that mean? It's not a person trespassing on your property. It's about how to deal with any transgression that would cause you to be angry, resentful, hateful, and to seek revenge. Someone stole from you, lied, or cut you off in traffic. Someone at work took your idea and presented it as their own.

You end up carrying that resentment and anger around like a marathon runner with a bag of bricks on their back. You forgive that person, not to let them off the hook for their transgression, but to remove the bag of bricks from your back. It's how you achieve peace of mind. It's about rewiring our brains.

Lead us not into temptation but deliver us from evil. What does that mean? We know the word evil means bad things that fall on the negative side of the leadership lifeline. We shouldn't be tempted to seek material things to achieve happiness, to lust after things, or to act greedily.

If the universe or a higher power has absolute laws, we should seek to live in the same manner—not to live perfectly but to progress toward a more positive life.

Let's look at the prayer of Intercession, asking for something for others. It is also about speaking positive things about others, such as encouraging our children. Remember, passages can address multiple lessons. Chapter 18 in the Book of Proverbs is not just about ourselves.

> *From the fruit of their mouth a person's stomach is*
>     *filled; with the harvest of their lips they are*
>     *satisfied.*
> *The tongue has the power of life and death,*
>     *and those who love it will eat its fruit.*
>           ~Proverbs 18:20-21 (NIV)

Our children are our seeds in the literal sense. We planted them. The type of person they become as adults is the harvest being reaped. How they grow will be determined by what they are exposed to in life. We are the gardeners. We have to provide fertilizer and sunshine while doing our best to keep the weeds out of their minds. The weeds are the negative thoughts that drown out the positive thoughts, just like weeds will overtake a flower garden.

It's not all about positive reinforcement. We call it "tough love." Humans are naturally rebellious. If you love your children, you protect them from others and from doing stupid stuff. Speaking words over others is not all about being nicey-nicey. Speaking the truth can sometimes seem like we're being mean.

The first Book of Corinthians, chapter 13, verses 4 through 7, describes love. This passage includes the language "It always protects." Then, the Book of Proverbs, chapter 13, verse 24, uses the hyperbole of "hate" to highlight the extreme importance of disciplining our children.

*Love is patient, love is kind. It does not envy, it does not boast, it is not proud. It does not dishonor others, it is not self-seeking, it is not easily angered, it keeps no record of wrongs. Love does not delight in evil but rejoices with the truth. It always protects, always trusts, always hopes, always perseveres.*
~1 Corinthians 13:4-7 (NIV)

*Whoever spares the rod hates their children, but the one who loves their children is careful to discipline them.*
~Proverbs 13:24 (NIV)

Disciplining children is an act of love. We view love as an emotion, In the literary sense it is. However, all types of love require action.

Again, people think that praying is all about religion and that they have to be religious to pray. When we gain insight, we know that all of the different types of prayer are methods we use today. We have given them other names, affirmations, and meditation. Prayers and praying address behaviors that align with and do not align with acting in leadership and being a leader.

I challenge you to find passages in the *Bible* that address these six types of prayer. You may even find a kind of prayer I did not list here.

# CHAPTER SEVENTEEN

# Anxiety, Worry, and Stress

In the previous chapter, Meditation, Affirmation, and Prayer, we addressed how people think that praying is all about religion and that they have to be religious to pray. Almost everyone uses some form of prayer today. We just don't call it praying; we use labels such as meditation and affirmation.

According to the American Psychological Association, psychologists have found that mindfulness meditation positively affects our brain and biology, improving mental and physical health. Benefits include lower blood pressure, more emotional control, improved sleep quality, less age-related memory loss, increased critical thinking, and less stress and anxiety.

I frequently discuss synonyms in my books. A synonym is a word or phrase that means exactly or nearly the same as another word or phrase in the same language. When we combine the multiple synonyms the *Bible* uses to address the human conditions of anxiety, worry, and stress, we find over 300 references.

The language includes words like heaviness, distress, our cares, our troubles, concerns, unease, doubt, nervousness, and fear. Of course, depending on the translation, we can see the actual words anxiety and worry.

In the Book of John, chapter 14, the NIV version, the first line is, "Do not let your hearts be troubled. "That statement means exactly what it sounds like, "don't worry, don't be anxious."

Your mind is praying every single day; it's just doing it on autopilot. Every thought you have is a form of affirmation. We have the choice to direct those thoughts or not direct them.

According to Dr. Bruce Lipton, who wrote *The Biology of Belief,* the subconscious mind processes information at 40 million bits per second, and our conscious mind processes information at 40 bits per second. Therefore, our subconscious mind operates in the background, controlling 95% to 99% of our daily actions and doing this "on autopilot." Our subconscious easily overrides our conscious mind, and we are unaware that it is happening.

I don't know about you, but I would like two things:

1) To understand how to be more in control of my subconscious mind and

2) non-medical or drug-induced ways to lower my blood pressure, have more emotional control, improve my sleep quality, have less age-related memory loss, increase my critical thinking, and sure as heck have less stress and anxiety in my life.

Again, this is not about completely ridding ourselves of stress, anxiety, doubt, or fears. It is a lifelong progression of a worthy ideal.

According to the National Institute for Mental Health, occasional anxiety is a normal part of life. We commonly worry about things such as health, money, or family problems. When anxiety escalates beyond what is considered normal, then it gets labeled as a disorder. If you think you need help, seek a professional.

Chapter 6 of the Book of Matthew is part of the TED Talk that Jesus gave in front of a large crowd. It's the Sermon on the Mount. Near the beginning, Jesus talks about prayer and then shortly thereafter provides a lesson on worry. Let's look at the lesson.

*Do Not Worry*

*Therefore I tell you, do not worry about your life, what you will eat or drink; or about your body, what you will wear. Is not life more than food, and the body more than clothes? Look at the birds of the air;*

*they do not sow or reap or store away in barns, and
yet your heavenly Father feeds them. Are you not
much more valuable than they? Can any one of you
by worrying add a single hour to your life?*

*And why do you worry about clothes? See how the
flowers of the field grow. They do not labor or
spin. Yet I tell you that not even Solomon in all his
splendor was dressed like one of these. If that is
how God clothes the grass of the field, which is here
today and tomorrow is thrown into the fire, will he
not much more clothe you—you of little faith? So do
not worry, saying, "What shall we eat?" or "What
shall we drink?" or "What shall we wear?" For the
pagans run after all these things, and your heavenly
Father knows that you need them. But seek first his
kingdom and his righteousness, and all these things
will be given to you as well. Therefore do not worry
about tomorrow, for tomorrow will worry about
itself. Each day has enough trouble of its own.*
~Matthew 6:25-34 (NIV)

We worry about what others think of our clothing
style. Am I up to date on the current fashion trends?
Fashion trends? This "I need to have the latest fashion"
is all made up propaganda by clothes designers to sell us
things. We focus on having big houses, owning lots of
fancy things, and then worry about people stealing our
precious stuff. Go ahead and try to convince me that

there's no irony in that vicious cycle. We accumulate so much crap that most of it sits unused, collecting dust.

What's our next step after accumulating tons of junk? We set parameters such as "if we haven't used it in two years, it's time to get rid of it." Then we either give it away or sell it for half or less of what we paid for it. My wife Lisa and I used to do that. Now we do the opposite. We ask the right questions up front. Is this a need or a want? Are we making this purchase to be fashionable or keep up with the neighbors? How often will we actually use it now and in one or two years? Does it have to be brand new, or can we get by with used? Then we remind ourselves of all the things we bought, only to get rid of them.

Do you compare yourself to others, worrying if you are good enough? Am I handsome or pretty compared to others? We constantly compare, yet it serves no purpose. We worry about being judged by others. The list of things we worry about is long, and all of them are addressed in the various books of the *Bible*.

Verse 27 at the end of the first paragraph says it all. "Can any one of you by worrying add a single hour to your life?" Not only is the answer a stern "no," but worrying takes hours away from our lives. Worry is a form of stress and anxiety.

Dr. Robert S. Eliot, M.D., created the Life Stress Simulation Laboratory at the University of Nebraska Medical Center. In the 1970s, the lab originated with an idea by one of Dr. Eliot's colleagues, James Buell. Together, working for over a year, they developed a practical and effective way to test the effects of stress on our cardiovascular system. They then built their new international headquarters, the Institute of Stress Medicine, in Denver, Colorado. They scientifically proved what stress does to our bodies and provided the remedies to reduce it. The *Bible* contains the same information.

According to the Centers for Disease Control and Prevention, heart disease is the leading cause of death for men and women in the United States. From 2018 to 2021, one person died every 33 seconds in the United States from cardiovascular disease. Heart disease costs the United States about $239.9 billion each year in 2018 and 2019. Stress and anxiety are slowly killing most of us. Not acting in leadership causes stress and anxiety. Learning to reduce both stress and anxiety is a component of acting in leadership. All the advice we get from modern science has existed in the *Bible* for thousands of years.

We can also reframe the concept of hell. Wouldn't a hellish life be one full of anxiety, worry, and stress? Wouldn't living a life full of anger and resentment be a hellish life? A heavenly world is one without anxiety.

Why do we worry so much about things that should not matter? We need to reframe our misconceptions about the material world. You would never go to a high-end restaurant and say, "I'd like the fertilizer tail, please."

Up until the mid-to-late 1800s, Native Americans and early colonists used lobster as farming fertilizer and bait.

Before people began farming the oceans for these yummy crustaceans, lobsters would pile up on the shores by the hundreds—only servants ate them, not the well-to-do.

Upon dying, lobster innards rot quickly, especially the tail meat, making it inedible. This short window is why lobsters are shipped alive, or their tails are removed immediately and frozen.

Elites, those who thought themselves to be better than the poor, considered lobster something that people who were less than themselves ate. Idiots, the uneducated, and people of the lowest class status ate lobster.

In the mid-1800s, the inventions of canning food and transit railways provided a way to preserve lobster tail meat and transport it inland to non-coastal cities. Lobster became a cheap, easily transported, high-protein meal option.

Not only could products be transported by train, but so could people. Travel to coastal areas such as Maine became popular. People who were eating canned lobster now wanted to experience it fresh from the ocean. Zing, Zang, Zoom; lobster had become a new commodity instead of a nuisance, followed by a rise in recipe books on preparing lobster dishes.

In today's world, those of the so-called "elite status" can afford it, whereas the average person cannot. We pay big bucks for what was once used as fertilizer.

Why do we worry or have anxiety because others can afford to eat lobster, and we can't? It's fertilizer tail.

We do the same thing with clothing. Someone decided there's a new fashion trend, and having it makes you important and somehow more educated. Don't wear the latest fashion or the right fall colors? What a loser; you're an idiot; you should feel inadequate and anxious. This lesson warns us. "If that is how God clothes the grass of the field, which is here today and tomorrow is thrown into the fire, will he not much more clothe you— you of little faith?"

That fashion is here today and gone tomorrow. Then what? We chase that new fashion? We're easily manipulated by marketing. Or a commodity like lobster was once crap, and now it's cool and expensive. These are all materialistic concepts, all made up by mankind.

Next, the *Bible* does not say we should run around naked and starve. It states, "and your heavenly Father knows that you need them." We need clothes and food, but first, we must understand the universal principles and laws about envy, desire, hate, stress, and anxiety. When we do, we find that all this marketing regarding what we need is false. It's propaganda. It's manipulation.

Also, none of these lessons say we shouldn't be concerned. Being concerned about our kids' safety and doing our best to protect them is part of life. Remember, according to the National Institute for Mental Health, occasional anxiety is a normal part of life. It is normal for us to worry about things such as health, money, or family problems. When anxiety escalates beyond what is considered normal, then it gets labeled as a disorder.

Anxiety, worry, and fear all release reward and punishment chemicals into our bodies. Cortisol and adrenaline, in consistently large doses over time, damage our bodies. When we constantly worry and are anxious about things, we do not get the benefits of lower blood pressure, more emotional control, improved sleep quality, less age-related memory loss, and increased critical thinking.

Nature, the universe, First Cause, aka God, put the chemicals of cortisol and adrenaline in all of us. These chemicals illustrate the science behind the universal laws of acting in leadership. I love the 34th line from chapter six in the book of Matthew, "Therefore do not worry about tomorrow, for tomorrow will worry about itself. Each day has enough trouble of its own." These are words of wisdom.

Stress and anxiety are primarily self-inflicted. These undesirable emotional states come from knowing what is right and doing what is wrong. We know we shouldn't spend more than we make or have; it leads to being in debt. We know we shouldn't eat crappy; it leads to being unhealthy. We know we shouldn't mistreat others; it leads to unhealthy relationships. We shouldn't compare ourselves to others; it leads to anxiety. We shouldn't try to create happiness through material things; it's temporary and fades. Because it's temporary and fades, we seek more and more, escalating the accumulation of material things in a never-ending, futile cycle.

Let me repeat this: That does not mean we cannot have material things. I have material things, some very nice things. The *Bible* does not say anywhere that we cannot have them. It says not to put our hopes, joy, happiness, and faith in these things. Constantly striving to do so at excessive levels creates stress, anxiety, fear, guilt, shame, and other issues that go against the natural principles and laws of the universe.

The bag of bricks on our backs is loaded with anxiety, stress, fear, guilt, shame, and doubt. That's a heavy bag, folks. The Book of John, chapter 14, says,

> *All this I have spoken while still with you. But the Advocate, the Holy Spirit, whom the Father will send in my name, will teach you all things and will remind you of everything I have said to you. Peace I leave with you; my peace I give you. I do not give to you as the world gives. Do not let your hearts be troubled and do not be afraid.*
> ~John 14:25-27 (NIV)

John was one of the twelve original apostles. Remember, apostle means "messenger." John and his brother James were nicknamed Sons of Thunder. They were quick to anger, and if someone insulted them, violence was often the answer. James wrote down the lessons that Jesus taught him. Quick to anger is not a good trait to have when your job is to become a messenger that teaches the lessons of acting in leadership.

Let's deconstruct and reconstruct; let's reframe the language. An apostle is a messenger, and a disciple is a student. Jesus taught his students the lessons of acting in leadership so they could share those lessons with others. Next, let's put this passage from John in language we would see in a modern-day leadership presentation.

> *When our teacher was alive, he taught us this lesson. He understood that this lesson is a binding principle from the First Cause, a universal law that applies to everyone. You do not achieve contentment by acquiring material things. You deal with worry through meditation and affirmations to achieve peace of mind. If you follow these teachings, worry, anxiety, and fear will dissipate.*

John 14:24 says, "These words you hear are not my own; they belong to the Father who sent me." Humans are a result of the match that lit the Big Bang. Like everything else that exists, we are a creation of the universe. Jesus is a son of the universe, and he understood the universal laws of the creator.

Is the concept of a First Cause and the universal laws of life starting to make more sense now? It took me a while to get there, too. Let me explain why. There are four main personality types: Dominance, Influence, Steadiness, and Conscientiousness. These are known as the DISC personality profiles. The traits are...

D: Direct, firm, strong-willed, forceful
I: Outgoing, enthusiastic, optimistic, high-spirited

S: Even-tempered, accommodating, patient, humble

C: Analytical, reserved, precise, systematic.

We are all a little bit of each, but we are all dominant in one or two of the personality types. I score high in the "C" category. I lean toward being analytical, precise, and systematic. Because I am dominant in the "C" quadrant, I tend to be more skeptical of things. If you are an "I" personality, you might jump right in and say, "Yep, there's a creator, and I do not need all the research to confirm my beliefs." Not so much in my case.

When we see verses that talk about how God will punish us or reward us, we think in terms of being struck down or some other catastrophic thing. Let's look at the Book of Romans, chapter 2, verses 5 through 11. First, we will outline who wrote it, to whom it was written, and why it was written.

- ✓ Paul wrote the Book of Romans.
- ✓ Romans 2 was one of a series of letters to the Roman church.
- ✓ Paul wrote the letters because he saw that the church was straying off course.
- ✓ Those letters illustrated the universal principles the church should focus on to get back on the right path.

*But because of your stubbornness and your unrepentant heart, you are storing up wrath against yourself for the day of God's wrath, when his*

*righteous judgment will be revealed. God "will repay each person according to what they have done." To those who by persistence in doing good seek glory, honor and immortality, he will give eternal life. But for those who are self-seeking and who reject the truth and follow evil, there will be wrath and anger. There will be trouble and distress for every human being who does evil: first for the Jew, then for the Gentile; but glory, honor and peace for everyone who does good: first for the Jew, then for the Gentile. For God does not show favoritism.*
~Romans 2:5-11 (NIV)

What does "storing up wrath" mean? What does "his righteous judgment" mean? I've never seen any wrath or righteous judgment doled out to anyone, have you? No person I've ever spoken to has. That is, until we reframe it. Let's rewrite in modern-day language.

*Anger, hate, worry, anxiety, and many other things dump excessive levels of cortisol and adrenaline into our bodies. Eventually, they will cause permanent damage. The universe put this behavioral mechanism into all of us. The universe will repay each of us according to what we have done. The universe does not discriminate.*

Ahhhh, the little light bulb goes on over our heads. The universe punishes and rewards us for certain behaviors using a condition-based computer program.

An 'If-then" statement in computer science refers to a conditional statement that executes an outcome based on whether a specific condition is true or false.

If you act immorally, then you feel guilty. If you get angry, then cortisol gets released into your body. If you help someone, then oxytocin gets released into your body. These are all "if A, then B" conditional outcomes. They are not random. They are intentional; by design.

It reminds me of the movie *Road House*. Patrick Swayze plays the character Dalton, a bouncer who studies the mind-calming techniques of martial arts. One of the bouncers he is training asks him, "How will we know when it's time not to be nice?" Dalton responds, "You won't. I'll tell you."

We have chemicals in our bodies that tell us when we are not acting rightly, which means we are not acting in leadership. We don't get to make up our own rules that contradict these foundational principles and universal laws.

The New Century Version (NCV) translation is more specific. The modern translation would be, "God will reward or punish every person for what that person has done." We see that the language of "repay" encompasses both reward and punishment. Therefore, we could also reframe it to include the reward chemicals.

> *Anger, hate, worry, anxiety, and many other things dump cortisol and adrenaline into our bodies. These things accumulate. Eventually, they will do permanent damage. Love,*

*generosity, patience, calmness, and all the other good qualities of mankind release oxytocin, dopamine, and serotonin into our bodies. These things extend your life. The universe put these behavioral mechanisms into all of us. The universe will repay each of us according to what we have done. The universe does not discriminate.*

We do not get to make up our own rules. However, we can decide whether to follow these universal principles and laws. That's where "free will" comes into play. The science behind these universal chemicals is now common knowledge. The science was unknown then, but people could see the effects of certain behaviors.

We can feel guilt and shame, but we also get a warm and fuzzy feeling from helping others. Part of what we feel is due to the release of these chemicals. Long ago, people could not explain it in scientific terms, but they were undoubtedly aware of it and could see its impact.

All of this brings us back to the premise of this book you are reading right now. The *Bible* teaches acting in leadership. These built-in behavioral reward and punishment mechanisms exist by design. They help us identify universal principles and laws to define the difference between right and wrong, good and bad, moral and immoral. To define when we are acting in leadership.

# CHAPTER EIGHTEEN

# Sign, Sign, Everywhere A Sign

Show me a sign. What do you mean by sign? Most people can't answer that question. What would a sign look like?

The behavioral chemicals cortisol, oxytocin, dopamine, and serotonin are signs. In chapter twelve, we learned that by age 3, before children are capable of any sophisticated moral reasoning, we have the emotional perception of "wrongness" through guilt and shame. Those are signs that we have acted wrongly.

We have to look for them. It's like driving down the road lost when there are signs all around you. You have tunnel vision, never turning your head to look for them. If you're not looking for them, you will never see them. When I learned to drive, they taught us to slow down to make sure we don't miss signs, and to ensure we can read them clearly. If you are not looking for signs, you will never see one.

Sadly, human behaviors often follow technology. When we drive now, we don't even have to look for signs. Some computer programs tell us where to go, so we stop looking.

That transition from looking for road signs to being told where to go is not far from how massive amounts of behavioral marketing tell us how we should live and what will theoretically make us happy. Most people today have never been introduced to the rules of life, the Book of Life, or the lessons for acting in leadership.

"Hey, universe, show me a sign." How about guilt when you do something that lacks integrity? That's a sign. What kind of sign? It is one that tells a person the difference between good and evil, right and wrong, moral and immoral.

In the Book of Matthew, chapter 16 talks about people not looking for any signs.

> He replied, "When evening comes, you say, 'It will be fair weather, for the sky is red,' and in the morning, 'Today it will be stormy, for the sky is red and overcast.' You know how to interpret the appearance of the sky, but you cannot interpret the signs of the times. A wicked and adulterous generation looks for a sign, but none will be given it except the sign of Jonah." Jesus then left them and

*went away.*

~Matthew 16:2-4 (NIV)

This *Bible* passage incorporates a great analogy. The phrase, "Red sky at night, sailor's delight. Red sky in the morning, sailor take warning," is still uttered today. Like the Pharisees that Jesus was speaking to, they thought they could see the signs of good and bad weather, yet they could not see the signs of good and bad behavior happening right in front of them at that very moment.

Did you happen to catch that this passage contained the language "the sign of Jonah?" Remember the story of Jonah from chapter five? Jonah felt guilty because he didn't take action and stand up against all the nasty crap going on in the city of Nineveh.

All kinds of terrible things were going on around the Pharisees. Jesus informed them, and they weren't doing anything about it. They could not see what was happening right now, the sign of the times. The *Bible* hammers us with the same lessons over and over. There aren't really that many lessons, but they look like a lot because the same lessons are presented in many ways.

We utter phrases like, "It is the right thing to do," but we have no idea what that means or where it came from. The first Book of Peter, chapter 3, verses 13 through 17, talks about doing the right things.

*Who is going to harm you if you are eager to do good? But even if you should suffer for what is right, you are blessed. Do not fear their threats; do not be frightened. But in your hearts revere Christ as Lord. Always be prepared to give an answer to everyone who asks you to give the reason for the hope that you have. But do this with gentleness and respect, keeping a clear conscience, so that those who speak maliciously against your good behavior in Christ may be ashamed of their slander. For it is better, if it is God's will, to suffer for doing good than for doing evil.*

~1 Peter 3:13-17 (NIV)

This passage says to be prepared to give an answer. What's the answer? Because it's the right thing to do, that is a correct answer, but that answer does not provide a logical reason with evidence. Do you know what provides evidence? The behavior chemicals cortisol, adrenaline, oxytocin, dopamine, and serotonin, and the signals from the amygdala and hippocampus parts of our brain that activate guilt and shame.

This passage also tells us that it is better to suffer the remarks and threats of fools for acting rightly than to suffer the consequences of not acting rightly. A gang member approaches another teenager and entices him or her to join their gang. The kid says, "No." So, the gang member makes fun of them, calls them chicken, and says things to guilt them into joining. Perhaps they even hit them or harm them physically in some other way. This passage says it is better to endure physical harm than to suffer the consequences of stealing, hurting others, and perhaps even committing murder.

The movie *Gran Torino* with Clint Eastwood contains scenes of a teenage boy saying no to gang members trying to recruit him. Because he refuses, the gang members punish him and beat up his sister. They both endure the punishment of acting rightly over the punishment of acting wrongfully. Would you?

Most people say they would, but the reality of the world tells us just the opposite. The gang analogy easily makes the point. But what if you are asked to do something you know to be unethical at work? Would you stand up to it? What's the right thing to do? What's your reason for it being the right thing to do? Where does the concept of right and wrong come from?

The right thing to do is derived from a universal set of principles and laws that apply to everyone. Otherwise, how we should live our lives is just an opinion. I've provided evidence throughout this book of how the *Bible* teaches acting in leadership. Without that, it's just my opinion. If you argue against what I present, without evidence to the contrary, it's just your opinion.

How do we instinctively know what constitutes right and wrong? The behavior chemicals cortisol, oxytocin, dopamine, and serotonin guide us, as do the emotions of guilt and shame. It's a darn good start, and there's scientific evidence. Otherwise, it's just an opinion.

Opinions and excuses are like buttholes. We all have them, and they all stink. We know how to look for some signs now. But what about all that talk surrounding "hearing from God?"

I used to think the structure of the word "conscience" was odd. Now, I see it differently. It contains the word "science." Your conscience can trigger feelings of guilt, shame, or remorse when you act in ways that contradict universal moral laws or, conversely, feelings of satisfaction and pride when you act in accordance with a moral principle or universal law. It is often described as an internal voice or awareness that helps you distinguish between ethical and unethical, right and wrong.

An inner voice that speaks to us? Where have I seen that before? Oh yeah, in the *Bible*. The Book of Job (pronounced Jobe) is said to have been written by Moses or King Solomon.

> *Why do you complain to him*
> *that he responds to no one's words?*
> *For God does speak—now one way, now another—*
> *though no one perceives it.*
> *In a dream, in a vision of the night,*
> *when deep sleep falls on people*
> *as they slumber in their beds,*
> *he may speak in their ears*
> *and terrify them with warnings,*
> *to turn them from wrongdoing*
> *and keep them from pride,*
> ~Job 33:13-17 (NIV)

We know we have the inner voice of our conscience; that's one voice speaking to us. Who has a conscience? We all do. It's another built-in universal mechanism. It's a warning, just like a fire alarm in any building. We don't have to act on it. We can stay in the burning building. "For God does speak—now one way, now another—though no one perceives it."

This passage addresses not hearing the inner voice of our conscience. Not hearing our conscience is the same issue we have with not seeing signs; we have not learned to listen. Listen to your conscience; what does it tell you about lying, stealing, cheating, murdering, helping others, giving to charity, and being nice to others even when they are mean to you?

Universal principles and laws exist. Evidence is provided by the built-in mechanisms that release behavior chemicals, and the signals from the amygdala and hippocampus parts of our brain. This evidence helps us to define right and wrong, good and evil, moral and immoral. These principles and laws tell us when we are acting in leadership, and the lessons about them are provided in the *Bible*. The *Bible* teaches acting in leadership.

# CHAPTER NINETEEN

# Past, Present, and Future

The saying, "The past is history. The future is a mystery. Today is a gift, that's why it's called the present," is often attributed to Eleanor Roosevelt. What does this mean, and what is the source of this simple yet enlightening lesson?

## The Past

I lost count of the number of movies that illustrate lessons about living in the past. One of the more common themes is how the high school sports hero continues to relive their "glory days" or that "one big play" that won the championship game. These people are stuck in the past. They think their best days are behind them, so they can't fully live in the present.

Not only do many people live in the past of their own life, they live in someone else's past, reliving the glory days of other people. In the movie *Sweet Home Alabama*, Jake is the former high school quarterback who makes the big play to win the championship game. However, it is not him reliving that moment; his high school buddies all want him to remember it. They constantly say, "Hey Jake, remember the big game." He wants nothing to do with the story anymore because he has moved on, and they haven't.

Getting stuck on past successes is bad, but the real tragedy is that we get stuck on the bad things that have transpired in our lives. We cannot reconcile with that past. We beat ourselves up and do not forgive ourselves.

> *Therefore, if anyone is in Christ, the new creation has come: The old has gone, the new is here! All this is from God, who reconciled us to himself through Christ and gave us the ministry of reconciliation: that God was reconciling the world to himself in Christ, not counting people's sins against them. And he has committed to us the message of reconciliation.*
> ~2 Corinthians 5:17-19

When we reconcile with our past, we feel complete. When something is complete, we move on. "The old has gone, the new is here." We can learn lessons from the past, but we cannot stay stuck there.

That's a great lesson, but what remedy allows a person to move on? The answer is found in the first Book of John, chapter 1, verses 8 – 9.

*If we claim to be without sin, we deceive ourselves
and the truth is not in us. If we confess our sins, he
is faithful and just and will forgive us our sins and
purify us from all unrighteousness.*
~ 1 John 1:8-9 (NIV)

We have to forgive ourselves. Remember, to confess something is to admit it, to take ownership and responsibility. We use the same solution to move on when someone has done something to us: We forgive them. In chapter fourteen, Meditations, Affirmations, and Prayer, we already discussed this lesson. The solutions for forgiving ourselves and forgiving others are illustrated in the Our Father Prayer. We must also not repeat the bad things we did.

The language of the Book of Isaiah vividly describes how living in the past is like being lost in a wilderness wasteland. You must make your way through that wasteland.

*Forget the former things;
do not dwell on the past.
See, I am doing a new thing!
Now it springs up; do you not perceive it?
I am making a way in the wilderness
and streams in the wasteland.*
~Isaiah 43:18-19 (NIV)

The following passage in the Book of Luke is named "The Cost of Following Jesus." This parable teaches multiple lessons. Read the passage, and then I'll share the lessons.

> *As they were walking along the road, a man said to him, "I will follow you wherever you go."*
>
> *Jesus replied, "Foxes have dens and birds have nests, but the Son of Man has no place to lay his head."*
>
> *He said to another man, "Follow me."*
>
> *But he replied, "Lord, first let me go and bury my father."*
>
> *Jesus said to him, "Let the dead bury their own dead, but you go and proclaim the kingdom of God."*
>
> *Still another said, "I will follow you, Lord; but first let me go back and say goodbye to my family."*
>
> *Jesus replied, "No one who puts a hand to the plow and looks back is fit for service in the kingdom of God."*
>
> ~ Luke 9:57-62 (NIV)

This passage is based on a real-life event and is also a parable that contains at least four lessons.

1. Living a life of acting in leadership has challenges. It can be uncomfortable.
2. There are always trade-offs in life. We must give up something to make room for something new. If we want to be healthy, we must give up foods that are bad for us. We must leave those things behind.

3. It's about not making excuses to get started immediately. You do it right now. Not later. You go to the cupboard and throw away the half-box of snack cakes. You don't say, "Right after I eat this last half box, then I'll get started."

4. If you keep looking backward into the past, you cannot see what you are doing right now or what's right in front of you. The fruits of your labor are forward.

## The Present

Because modern technology constantly distracts us, nothing could be more relevant than the lesson about how "the present is a gift."

> *This is the day the LORD has made;*
> *We will rejoice and be glad in it.*
> ~Psalm 118:24 (NKJV)

You could be at work, in a meeting, watching a movie, talking with your spouse or a friend, or driving your car, then "beep" or "ding" goes your phone. "What am I missing?" races through your mind. "It must be important."

It reminds me of the Pixar movie *UP*. A grumpy old man, Carl Fredricksen, and a young boy named Russell, who has a positive outlook on life, take a journey to Paradise Falls. When they arrive, they encounter a dog wearing a collar that verbalizes his thoughts. His name is Doug.

Doug is having conversations with Carl and Russell, then suddenly gets distracted. He snaps his head to one side and says, "Squirrel." In another scene, he is distracted, turns his head, and says, "Ball." Our dog Lily is a Jack Russell Terrier. There is no relation to the boy character named Russell, just in case you were distracted by that thought. Lily, our dog, is constantly distracted by everything.

If you are constantly distracted by little things, especially the little beeps and dings on your mobile device, congratulations, you have the same level of focus as Doug and Lily. Analogies are wonderful things. I just compared your ability to "focus on the now" to a pair of Dogs, one of which isn't even real. Dogs cannot help it. What is our excuse?

In the 1980s, we used to plan three-day canoe and camping trips down the St. Croix River. This river creates part of the border between Minnesota and Wisconsin. Most of it is protected land, so it's a wilderness without many homes or access to anything.

At times, we'd have over 30 people on these adventures. We brought horseshoes and a professional-level beach volleyball setup. People went swimming, fished the river, played volleyball, tossed horseshoes, and sat around the campfire chatting and telling stories. Because we were fully engaged in the "now," we never felt like we were missing out on something that was happening somewhere else. We were right where we wanted to be and, oftentimes, right where we needed to be.

We address this today as FOMO, Fear Of Missing Out. Even if we are not dwelling in the past or looking to the future, we wander off the path of life by thinking about something else, somewhere else.

The *Bible* is filled with stories of people with real-life struggles, just like you and me. Technology changes the environment in which we live, but it does not change the foundational components of how life works or how we live life by following a universal blueprint. We think it's somehow different now than it was over the thousands of years that humans have existed. What I have done is discover a way to lay out the blueprint that illustrates how acting in leadership was not different thousands of years ago, and it will not be different a thousand years from now.

People have lived and survived for centuries without cell phones. I'm not anti-cell phones or technology. I have one, but I do not let it control my life. Also, do not confuse this story with me living in the past. It's just an example of how technology can keep us from being fully engaged in what we are doing right now. Technology is not going anywhere, so we need to learn not to let it control us. This worthy ideal is accomplished through self-control.

The *Bible* warns us that if we do not have self-control, we will be slaves to what controls us: food, lust, money, material things, modern technology, and the fear of missing out. We learned how passages can teach a multitude of lessons. In chapter sixteen, Anxiety, Worry, and Stress, we used a passage from the Book of Matthew. This passage also addresses FOMO, a specific type of anxiety and worry.

*Do Not Worry*

*Therefore I tell you, do not worry about your life, what you will eat or drink; or about your body, what you will wear. Is not life more than food, and the body more than clothes? Look at the birds of the air; they do not sow or reap or store away in barns, and yet your heavenly Father feeds them. Are you not much more valuable than they? Can any one of you by worrying add a single hour to your life?*

*And why do you worry about clothes? See how the flowers of the field grow. They do not labor or spin. Yet I tell you that not even Solomon in all his splendor was dressed like one of these. If that is how God clothes the grass of the field, which is here today and tomorrow is thrown into the fire, will he not much more clothe you—you of little faith? So do not worry, saying, "What shall we eat?" or "What shall we drink?" or "What shall we wear?" For the pagans run after all these things, and your heavenly Father knows that you need them. But seek first his kingdom and his righteousness, and all these things will be given to you as well. Therefore do not worry about tomorrow, for tomorrow will worry about*

*itself. Each day has enough trouble of its own.*
~Matthew 6:25-34 (NIV)

Companies have had to go to extremes to address distractions in the workplace. One solution has been to place a wicker basket in the meeting room and have everyone put their phones in it. No one gets their phone back until the meeting is over. It's pretty hilarious when one of the phones starts vibrating, and the whole basket dances on the table, or someone forgets to turn off their ringer, and it's a duck quacking or a series of fart noises.

What is so dang important? What do we think we'll miss if we detach from our phones for an hour? FOMO has us bound in chains. Trust me, no matter what position you hold in any company, the company will not crumble if you turn off your phone for an hour. Nor will your life crumble if you do not know what Billy or Shelly are doing right at this very moment through their post on social media.

I have been in meetings with CEOs and Presidents of companies discussing strategies, and while I'm speaking to them, they pick up their phones and look at them. They always apologize, saying something like, "Sorry, go on" or "Sorry, where were we?" Then they do what? They give an excuse. Remember, we all have one, and they all stink.

It used to annoy me. Now, whether in business or life in general, I smile and laugh. When someone does this, the scenes from the movie *Up* are playing in my head. I see them as Doug, the distracted dog. I think I'll start bringing a tennis ball to meetings, holding it up in the air, and swinging my arm back and forth to see who locks onto it like Doug, the dog. I'll laugh as their heads twist side to side like they are watching a ping-pong match.

The lesson isn't just about not living in the past or future, but also about not being somewhere else in your mind. It's about being present in the present.

## The Future

> *Today is the tomorrow you worried about yesterday.*
> ~Dale Carnegie

That sums it all up, doesn't it? That is a vicious cycle and a horrible way to live. You spent yesterday thinking about and worrying about tomorrow. Now, tomorrow is here; it's today.

Will you waste another day thinking about another tomorrow? To continue thinking about tomorrow is not a good thing. You will miss life because life goes fast, like a mist that appears for a little while, then it vanishes.

> *Why, you do not even know what will happen tomorrow. What is your life? You are a mist that appears for a little while and then vanishes.*
> ~James 4:14 (NIV)

This does not mean we do not plan. The *Bible* contains plenty of passages using the word "plan" and multiple parables about planning.

> *The plans of the diligent lead to profit*

*as surely as haste leads to poverty.*
~Proverbs 21:5 (NIV)

We think of profit and poverty in terms of money. It can be, but this lesson is about how we live our lives. If I do not plan to eat healthily, I put my body into a poverty of health. If I do not plan to train my mind to have positive thoughts, I put my mind into a poverty of negativity. If I do not handle my finances well, I can literally put myself into debt and financial poverty. If I do not plan to have good relationships, I live in relationship poverty.

Benjamin Franklin is often attributed to the adage, "If you fail to plan, you plan to fail." In his autobiography, Franklin described himself as a deist. Deism is believing in a God who created the universe but does not intervene in its affairs. The earliest printing I could find that states this principle is from the periodical *The Biblical World* (1919). I'm pretty sure we know where this Reverend found the lesson.

*If you fail to prepare, you are preparing to fail.*
~ Reverend H. K. Williams, The Biblical World

We must be diligent in planning and preparing for all areas of our lives, including the final scene of our personal stage play: departing this world. It's okay to plan, but haste is not a progression; it refers to a type of escalation. We covered this in chapter thirteen.

In Proverbs 21:5 above, "haste" means we live in a state of constant rush because we try to pack so many things into our lives. We dash around, driving kids to three sports, working late hours to become wealthier as fast as we can. We've escalated our lives. Suddenly, life passes us by. What areas of your life have suffered because you live this way? Your health? Your friendships? Your time to shut down and relax? Are you putting any of these areas of your life into poverty?

I'll be 64 years old when this book is published. Yes, it would be wonderful if someone had taught me these lessons early in life. But that is not the case. I began to learn them around 50 years of age. It's never too late to start. Now, I do my best not to dwell on the past. I do not get stuck thinking about what I could have done differently. But I do use my past experiences not to repeat doing stupid things. It doesn't always work. I do not get distracted by the little beeps and dings of my phone when I'm engaged in any activity, and I do not worry about what tomorrow will bring. I plan and prepare, so I do not have to worry.

I learned these lessons from the personal development era and modern-day leadership teachings. What I discovered is that the *Bible* contains all of the lessons.

> *Therefore do not worry about tomorrow, for tomorrow will worry about itself. Each day has enough trouble of its own.*
> ~Matthew 6:34 (NIV)

If we put this verse into modern-day language, it would read like this...

> *Dude! Why are you constantly talking about tomorrow instead of focusing on what needs to be done today? Plenty is going on right now. Let's focus on that stuff.*

Because I follow these lessons, which are universal principles and laws from a First Cause, I am more content than ever in life. This contentment is not based on what I have but on how I live, which is by acting in leadership. The *Bible* addresses "being at peace" over 400 times. Do you wish you had more peace in your life?

That last statement sounds more biblical than leadership-based. Yet, all the lessons presented in this chapter are taught in modern-day leadership coaching platforms, and they all address how we can achieve more peace of mind by not dwelling on the past, living in the future, and constantly being distracted today. If you are following this advice and implementing these practices, then you are already following the teachings of the *Bible*.

Dr. Harold Ivan Smith wrote *Eleanor: A Spiritual Biography*. When describing Eleanor Roosevelt, Dr. Smith states, "She was very public about her faith. In hundreds of 'My Day' and 'If You Ask Me' columns, she addressed issues of faith, prayer, and the *Bible*." One of Eleanor's many famous quotes is based on biblical lessons.

> *"The past is history. The future is a mystery. Today is a gift; that's why it's called the present."*

CHAPTER TWENTY

# Final Chapter

I could continue providing chapter after chapter on how the *Bible* teaches acting in leadership. I'm sitting here looking at my collection of books, hundreds of them, all illustrating one or more of the foundational principles and universal laws about how we behave and how a person conducts oneself.

Two of these books address habits: *The Power of Habit* by Charles Duhigg and *Atomic Habits* by James Clear. People seeking to become leaders attend seminars that address developing the right habits.

A habit is a pattern of behavior. Both books, *The Power of Habit* and *Atomic Habits,* provide methods for developing positive habits. No leadership platform encourages people to develop bad habits. Both books discuss how our little actions accumulate to the point of having a major impact on our lives. We saw this lesson in the Parable of the Mustard Seed.

*Though it is the smallest of all seeds, yet when it grows, it is the largest of garden plants and becomes a tree, so that the birds come and perch in its branches.*

~Matthew 13:32 (NIV)

The lessons of acting in leadership are all around us. We see them in movies and literature. But we get sidetracked with other things. We search to see if the person who wrote the book or made the movie is connected to some religious faith. I have done this.

For instance, people argue whether the concept of good and evil in the *Star Wars* movie series is religion-based. One person says, "See, George Lucas says he's not religious. Therefore, the concept of the dark side of the force is not based on biblical lessons." Then another person says, "Yeah, well, C.S. Lewis wrote *The Chronicles of Narnia*, and his life has led him to believe in a higher power."

The Harry Potter and Marvel movie series are some of my favorites. All of the films in both series contrast right and wrong. The D.C. Comics movie series illustrates the same lessons and principles.

Pixar and DreamWorks both have the lessons of acting in leadership embedded in the storylines of most movies. The great part is that most of them include adult-based humor. Grown-ups watch them as much as kids.

J. R. R. Tolkien was a devout Roman Catholic from boyhood, and he described *The Lord of the Rings* as a "fundamentally religious and Catholic work; unconsciously so at first, but consciously in the revision." See, I added a religious context to that last one. Whether a person is religious or not should not matter when it comes to acting in leadership.

We're focused on the wrong things. We should be asking, "What does it mean to act in leadership?" When we ask that question, the answers become apparent. Acting in leadership addresses the difference between right and wrong, good and bad, moral and immoral. But first, we need a standard for what constitutes right and wrong.

If there is no standard for right and wrong, good and evil, moral and immoral, then why do all these movies contain representations of right versus wrong, good versus evil? Where did the writers get these contrasting principles? And more importantly, why do they all teach the exact same lessons?

The lessons contained in all of these films come from the universal principles and laws that apply to everyone. These principles and laws define when a person is acting in leadership.

The foundational principles and universal laws for moral behaviors are supported by science in two primary ways:

1. The release of the chemicals cortisol, adrenaline, oxytocin, serotonin, and dopamine. These built-in universal chemicals are activated based on our behaviors. It's a

system that helps us define when we are acting in leadership.

2. The inherent, essential universal responses from our amygdala and hippocampus parts of our brain, which include guilt, shame, worry, anxiety, fear, love, joy, peace, and calm, are activated based on our behaviors. These built-in mechanisms help us define when we are acting in leadership.

Today, we have a much more detailed understanding of how and why things work. We understand why volcanoes erupt, hurricane winds hammer coastal cities, and earthquakes shake the ground, sending tsunamis across the ocean. We understand that long-term and short-term weather cycles happen on the planet—ice ages come and go. We have a greater understanding of why there are droughts and rainy cycles. Why lightning strikes trees and sets things on fire is no longer a mystery to us. We know why solar eclipses appear to make the Earth go dark, and lunar eclipses make the moon seem to disappear. We understand these things.

We also understand the science behind the chemicals cortisol, adrenaline, oxytocin, serotonin, and dopamine. We also have a much deeper scientific understanding of our amygdala and hippocampus parts of our brain, of guilt, shame, pride, and other emotions as they relate to human behaviors.

These concepts must have seemed mystical to everyone thousands of years ago. Today, we know and understand the science behind all of these things. Our deep understanding makes the *Bible* an incredible compilation of leadership lessons presented to us using interesting language and told in exciting ways.

I could write another book about how the *Dhammapada* teaches the lessons of acting in leadership. Look up the four noble truths, Dukka, Samuda, Nirodha, and Magga. The alignment between the four noble truths and the lessons of the *Bible* in terms of how we self-inflict with anxiety, stress, and worry is amazing.

I chose the *Bible* because it is the most complete and entertaining life manual from thousands of years ago. It is a library of 66 books written in times when life was quite different from what it is now.

I could not imagine what it would have been like to live thousands of years ago and then try to explain the scientifically supported things we understand today. They lived in different times but somehow understood these lessons, and the lessons have not changed.

Rather than writing an entire series of books that would explain how every passage of every book in the *Bible* teaches the lessons of acting in leadership, I am extending a challenge to my readers.

First, everyone falls into some belief category regarding religion. Here are the most common.

- Atheist (believes that no God of any sort exists)

- Deist (belief in a God who created the universe, but that this God does not intervene)
- Agnostic (a person who doesn't have a belief either way, for or against there being a God)
- Theist (believes there is a God).

No matter which category you fall into and whether you have read the *Bible* or not, I offer a challenge. Make a list of modern-day leadership traits and attributes, then find the books and passages in the *Bible* that illustrate the lessons associated with those traits and characteristics.

First, we need to revisit chapter three, "Foundational Principles of Leadership," to ensure we understand what acting in leadership means in its true essence. Here is a quick summary of what leadership is and is not.

---

Leadership is fundamentally about how we behave, how we act, and how we conduct ourselves. Most of the 1,000 modern-day leadership labels and definitions are not derived from the fundamentals of how we should live and behave.

Be sure you do not use any of the misguided leadership labels and definitions created by attaching leadership to ethnicity, race, gender, or other identity-based characteristics. Be sure you do not use any of the misguided labels or definitions created by attaching leadership to a position in any hierarchy or associated with the functions of operating a business.

---

I will also provide a list of the key points from my book, *There Is No Such Thing as Business Leadership.*

- There should be no such thing as a negatively based leadership attribute. For example, unethical leadership. These negatively based attributes are things that "do not" constitute acting in leadership.
- Leadership isn't influence or inspiration. These labels developed because we misguidedly attached leadership to a position in a hierarchy and studied leadership in terms of operating a business.
- Leadership isn't a position in any hierarchy. By default, this means only a very limited number of people can be leaders.
- Leadership does not require a person to have followers. At some point, we'd run out of followers, then, by default, no one can be a leader.
- There is no such thing as white leadership, black leadership, Hispanic leadership, Asian leadership, or any gender, ethnicity, or identity-based leadership. None of these things has anything to do with a person's ability to act in leadership.
- There is no such thing as political leadership, business leadership, authoritarian leadership, participative leadership, servant leadership,

transactional leadership, or transformational leadership. These categories and labels are created by attaching leadership to a position in a hierarchy and associating it with doing business. They do not relate to a person's ability to act in leadership.

I will get you started with a couple more examples: We say leaders do not "give up," and we say "they persevere." Where would you find those traits and attributes being addressed in the *Bible*? The Book of Galatians, chapter 9, verse 9. And the Book of James, chapter 1, verses 2 to 4.

> *Let us not become weary in doing good, for at the proper time we will reap a harvest if we do not give up.*    ~Galatians 6:9 (NIV)

> *Consider it pure joy, my brothers and sisters, whenever you face trials of many kinds, because you know that the testing of your faith produces perseverance. Let perseverance finish its work so that you may be mature and complete, not lacking anything.*
> ~James 1:2-4 (NIV)

Now it's your turn. Which passages of the *Bible* address the following traits and attributes associated with acting in leadership?

- Leaders work on self-awareness.
- Leaders work on emotional intelligence (EQ)
- Leaders are visionaries
- Leaders are trustworthy
- Leaders are strategic thinkers
- Leaders remain calm
- Leaders plan
- Leaders care about others.
- Leaders have courage (they overcome fear)
- Leaders have a willingness to change
- Leaders work on humility
- Leaders are humble
- Leaders take responsibility; they hold themselves accountable
- Leaders have a positive mindset
- Leaders are grateful
- Leaders are problem solvers
- Leaders are constantly learning
- Leaders are open-minded
- Leaders expect and plan for change
- Leaders show respect
- Leaders see challenges as an opportunity to grow

This list will get you started. You can look up as many leadership attributes as you want. Perhaps you have a favorite you want to practice that's not on this list. You'll notice that the above list contains mostly positive attributes. The traits and characteristics of acting in leadership are always contrasted by the things that "do not" represent acting in leadership. You can make a list of those as well and locate them. Anytime you have a non-leadership attribute, there is always a contrasting attribute that "is" a leadership attribute. Good cannot exist without evil. Right cannot exist without wrong. Moral cannot exist without immoral.

Remember, from chapter nine, you can reframe the language and passages into a modern-day leadership presentation format. Ask yourself how this might be presented if you attended a leadership presentation.

Ask yourself the following questions.

- ✓ Who wrote it?
- ✓ To whom did they write it?
- ✓ What was the purpose of writing it?
- ✓ What analogies, metaphors, and hyperbole were used?
- ✓ What do those analogies, metaphors, and hyperboles represent?
- ✓ What foundational principles and universal laws can you identify?
- ✓ What leadership behavior, attribute, or characteristic is the lesson addressing?

Once we deconstruct and reconstruct, and we reframe, the answers will appear. For instance, if the passage addresses fear, we know it is about overcoming fears or building courage or both. "Leaders have courage," and "leaders overcome their fears" are two universal principles and attributes of acting in leadership.

Often, a lesson or parable contains more than one leadership attribute. Multiple lessons combined in one passage can throw us off track.

The language back then did not contain all the words we use today. Language is continually expanding. Conduct multiple searches using today's language. The search results will provide passages that represent the behavior, attribute, or characteristic, but the *Bible* passage may not contain the actual language you used to search.

You must connect the dots as we did in Chapter 14. You deconstruct and reconstruct; reframe. Go back to chapter 14 and look at how I connected the dots for guilt-tripping using the passage in the Book of Philippians, chapter 2, verses 3 to 4. I constantly look up definitions and synonyms of words. Be prepared to do that often.

It will take practice, just like anything else. One of the best ways to get good at identifying the behaviors, attributes, and characteristics for acting in leadership in the *Bible* is to do it in a group. Make it a fun event. Have everyone bring a dish and discuss it over a meal. Once you get the hang of it, start deconstructing the most obscure passages you can find and then compare everyone's interpretations. You can gain a great deal of insight using this method.

As stated in the introduction, I wanted to convey two things through this book.

1.  There is a blueprint for acting in leadership that defines leadership in its true essence. Only when a person acts in leadership are they a leader.
2.  The *Bible* teaches acting in leadership. Leadership is fundamentally about how we behave; how we act; how a person conducts oneself. All of the foundational principles and universal laws, the attributes of acting in leadership, are illustrated in the *Bible*.

I believe I have accomplished both of those objectives. Second, I wanted to provide an easy and effective way for anyone to introduce the *Bible* to others by illustrating how the Bible teaches acting in leadership.

You now know that leadership has become a multi-billion-dollar industry. You also know that the desire for people to gain insight about the subject of leadership has increased dramatically. Sharing this book with others is a way to accomplish two objectives at the same time.

1)  Introduce them to what it means to act in leadership.
2)  Build a desire to learn how the Bible teaches acting in leadership.

I see the *Bible* in a very different light today than I did in my youth. I hope this book helps others to live a life of acting in leadership.

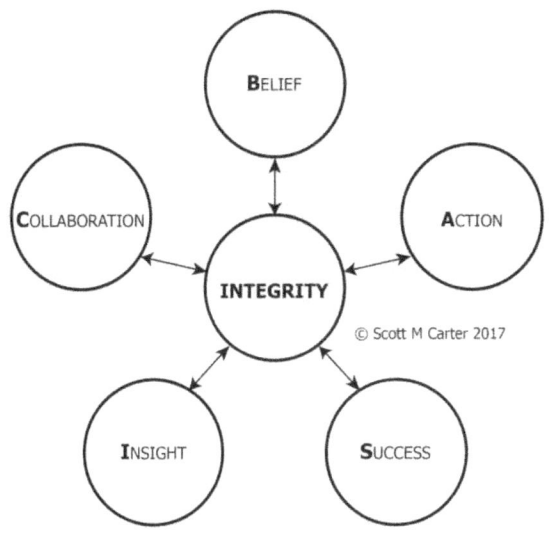

**Back to BASIC™**
Leadership Platform

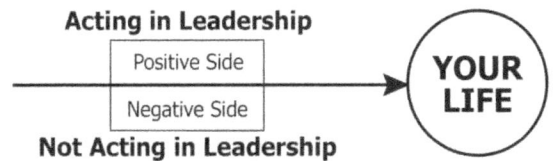

**Back to BASIC™**
Leadership Life Line